"In this delightful study of Augustine, doyen of church historians in the Americas, demonstrates the rich fruit of a lifetime of scholarly research. If one were to ask, how could anything new be said about Augustine?, González replies that it is the man's fundamental context that has so far been severely neglected. Augustine was a colonial author, well aware of his situation, poised in a tensile relation between the Numidian and Romano-Latin worlds, in an overextended empire that was coming to a crisis point in his own lifetime. This constitutes him, as González persuasively argues, as fundamentally a mestizo theologian: a man fixed in a tension of perspectives, origins, and goals that formed the energized background of his mind and work. After too many generations that have pretended Augustine was a white European, it is refreshing to read this elegant study of one of the giants of the Western Christian tradition."

John A. McGuckin, Columbia University, New York

"In a particularly insightful study, Justo González both introduces the breadth of St. Augustine's thought to modern readers and explains why his theology should be considered *mestizaje* (characterized by in-between-ness). Augustine—as both Roman and African, as a mediator between early Christianity and medieval Christianity—becomes a potent model for the many others, like González himself, who stand between worlds, cultures, and perspectives. It is a fine book."

Mark Noll, Francis A. McAnaney Professor of History emeritus, University of Notre Dame, author of *Protestantism: A Very Short History*

"I am deeply pleased to see the new book by Justo González on Augustine, which places him rightly in the African context. The author's theme of the crosscultural intricacies of Augustine's life illumines many other issues Christians face today. It is an extremely readable book by a distinguished church historian."

Thomas C. Oden, emeritus professor, Drew University, executive director, Center for Early African Christianity, general editor of the Ancient Christian Commentary on Scripture

"There are many fine introductions to Augustine's life and thought. But it is hard to think of one more timely for a new generation of readers than *The Mestizo Augustine*. With concise elegance and critical appreciation, Justo González recasts our imagination for Augustine's restless pilgrimage as the struggle and the wisdom of a mestizo. In doing so, he offers a compelling theological portrait of this massively influential figure of late antiquity and, importantly, of his continued relevance for our own era tempted by misplaced rage for purity."

Eric Gregory, Princeton University

"Justo L. González ranks among the most important and influential interpreters of Christian history in our era. *The Mestizo Augustine* is yet one more outstanding achievement. This groundbreaking study of Augustine offers compelling new insights into the life and thought of the great North African theologian and pastor from the perspective of *mestizaje* while advancing the overall project of *mestizaje* theology itself to a significant degree."

Dale T. Irvin, president and professor of world Christianity, New York Theological Seminary

"In a fresh, masterful, and highly readable way, Justo González shows the ongoing relevance and importance of the multicultural St. Augustine engaging his own contexts from a place between and within cultures. González provides new lenses for us to appreciate the mestizo Augustine as a resource for theology, ministry, and emerging ways of being church for our own contemporary multicultural, multiethnic, and globalized contexts in a racialized society."

Edwin David Aponte, executive director, Louisville Institute

"Justo González provides us with a unique and compelling retelling of the life of Augustine. He focuses on the *mestizajes* of Augustine's life to show us that his rich theology was born at the crossroads of peoples, languages, cultures, ethnicities, and social change. It is here that we encounter the deepest tensions of human existence but also where we can reflect most deeply on our understanding of God and our relationships with each other. We can thank González for reminding us through the life of Augustine that the *mestizajes* that we try to forestall or even deny 'may well be a sign of the future from which God is calling us.'"

Juan Francisco Martínez, vice president for diversity and international ministries, Fuller Theological Seminary

The MESTIZO AUGUSTINE

A Theologian Between Two Cultures

JUSTO L. GONZÁLEZ

IVP Academic

An imprint of InterVarsity Press
Downers Grove, Illinois

InterVarsity Press
P.O. Box 1400, Downers Grove, IL 60515-1426
ivpress.com
email@ivpress.com

InterVarsity Press® is the book-publishing division of InterVarsity Christian Fellowship/USA®, a movement of students and faculty active on campus at hundreds of universities, colleges and schools of nursing in the United States of America, and a member movement of the International Fellowship of Evangelical Students. For information about local and regional activities, visit intervarsity.org.

All Scripture quotations, unless otherwise indicated, are the author's translation.

Cover design: Cindy Kiple
Interior design: Beth McGill
Images: Historiated initial "I" depicting St. Augustine, Master of San Michele of Murano / Musee Marmottan
    Monet, Paris, France / Bridgeman Images

ISBN 978-0-8308-5150-8 (print)
ISBN 978-0-8308-7308-1 (digital)

Printed in the United States of America ♾

Library of Congress Cataloging-in-Publication Data
A catalog record for this book is available from the Library of Congress.

P 23 22 21 20 19 18 17 16 15 14 13 12 11 10 9 8 7 6 5 4 3 2 1

Y 35 34 33 32 31 30 29 28 27 26 25 24 23 22 21 20 19 18 17 16

To the many Latinas and Latinos

whose mestizaje has enriched mine.

Contents

Preface

I have been personally interested in Augustine for a long time. I was barely six or seven years old when the Bible societies launched a campaign under the theme of the famous words that Augustine heard in the garden in Milan: *tolle, lege*—take and read. Shortly thereafter I first heard the famous words that we have been created for God, and our hearts will be restless until they rest in God. Later, when as a zealous Protestant in Latin America I sought weapons against Roman Catholicism, I was told that in the writings of Augustine I would find many weapons. At about the same time the reading of Augustine's *Confessions* was for me both an inspiration and a challenge. Quite a few years later, when I was a student at Yale University, I was able to do some further and prolonged study of St. Augustine. And even more recently, in both personal and written dialogue with friends and companions such as Orlando Costas, Virgilio Elizondo, Ada Maria Isasi-Díaz, Daisy Machado and several others, I began to suspect that Augustine's restlessness was not due only to his distance from God, as he tells us in his *Confessions*, but also to the inner struggles of a person in whom two cultures, two legacies, two world visions clashed and mingled—in short, of a mestizo. It was this insight that led to the present book, which seeks to be a fairly simple introduction to Augustine's thought, but reading him from a perspective reflecting the context of a mestizaje similar to that which is experienced today in the United States by people of Spanish speech and Latino culture. This context is so unique and significant that I am told that soon the Royal Academy of the Spanish Language will include in its official dictionary the word *hispanounidense* (a strange compound word meaning something like "Hispanic United [States]ian"), since *hispanoamericano* is anyone born in the former colonies of Spain in America. The new term proposed to the academy reflects the experience of mestizaje that is so significant for us.

In the pages that follow I have not paid much attention to matters that are currently debated among specialists, and have also resisted the inclination to constantly quote secondary sources or scholarly works. Rather, I have tried to employ as much as possible the words of Augustine himself. Those other works and sources that I have not mentioned can easily be found on the Internet.

Finally, a word of gratitude not only to the friends and colleagues I have mentioned above but also to the two main companions that I have had in this task: Augustine himself through his works, and my wife, Catherine, professor emerita of church history at Columbia Theological Seminary, who has not only accompanied me in the task but also helped me understand Augustine himself. Thus, although sixteen centuries stand between them, both Augustine and Catherine speak in the pages that follow.

Abbreviation

NCP   The Works of Saint Augustine: A Translation for the 21st Century. Series edited by Boniface Ramsey. 50 vols. Hyde Park, NY: New City Press, 1990–.

Introduction

A Unique Theologian

Save Paul and the other New Testament writers, no other Christian writer or thinker has left such a profound footprint on the life and thought of the church as has St. Augustine. Certainly, this footprint is much more visible in Western Christianity—that is, Roman Catholicism and Protestantism—than in the Eastern churches, which are heirs of what in Augustine's time was the mostly Greek-speaking section of the Roman Empire. In the West, there is no theologian who can compare with Augustine. When the Germanic peoples invaded and eventually destroyed what had been the Roman Empire, Augustine and his writings served as a bridge between the former Christian tradition and the new context and cultures. Therefore it was through the eyes of Augustine that medieval Latin-speaking Christianity read Scripture and understood the Christian faith. When, a thousand years later, that Western Christianity was divided as a result of the Protestant Reformation, both sides in that great debate claimed the authority of Augustine in support of their views. To this day the vast majority of Christians, when they read, for instance, the epistles of Paul, do it, even unwittingly, through the eyes of Augustine.

Reading the New Testament or understanding the Christian faith through the eyes of Augustine is not necessarily wrong. But it is dangerous to do so without being aware of it, which makes us subject to or at least unaware followers of someone we do not know. Augustine can be very helpful, and indeed he is. But not to know him leads not only to a lack of understanding of our faith, but even to the inability to distinguish between the New Testament and what Augustine tells us the New Testament says. And the opposite is also true: a study of the life and thought of people in the past such as Augustine may well lead us to rediscover in our faith elements that the passing of centuries has obscured.

This is most important because, as we shall see, while Augustine made many valuable and important contributions to Christian theology, he also left us as a legacy many other elements that must be corrected.

Thus, in studying Augustine we do not do so out of mere antiquarian curiosity or historical interest—even though his life is as interesting as any novel—but also in quest of a deeper and fuller understanding of the faith that sustains us. In other words, we study Augustine not only for his past importance but also for his present relevance.

MESTIZAJE AND THEOLOGY

I have repeatedly stated that history is not just a narrative of the past, but is rather a reading and telling of that past in the light of our present. This means that when I study Augustine and his theology I do so in terms of who I am, how I understand myself, and the main concerns and interests not only of myself as an individual but also of the community to which I belong. Therefore Augustine is presented here through the lenses of a Christian and of a Christian community in the twenty-first century.

This does not mean that this is a falsified Augustine. It is not a matter of taking the past and reinventing it according to our own whims and desires. It is rather a question of looking at that past with new eyes, to see whether we find in it something that others, precisely because they did not have the same lenses, have not seen—or having seen, did not consider important.

In a few words, what I intend to explore here is the manner in which the perspectives and insights of Latino theology in our days—by which I mean theology done among that North American population of indigenous-Iberian-African origins who here are called "Hispanics" or "Latinos" and "Latinas"—may help us to see and rediscover in Augustine and in his theology some important elements that might otherwise not be noticed.

Likewise, I also hope that as we look at Augustine through Latino lenses he may become more relevant to our present-day context and challenges.

One of the characteristic themes of Latino/a theology—and of the social and ecclesiastical experience that forms its context—is mestizaje. This is a Spanish word that simply means being of mixed breed, and has traditionally been used in a pejorative way. However, in 1925 Mexican scholar and presidential candidate José Vasconcelos published an essay in which he claimed that mestizaje, rather than being a disadvantage or something to be bemoaned, is the future and the cutting edge of human civilization. According to Vasconcelos, what was happening in Latin America, particularly in Mexico, was that a new race was being born, one that included elements from all the races of the world, particularly the Indo-American, the European and the African. Over half a century later my friend and colleague Virgilio Elizondo took the insights of Vasconcelos as a way to name the experience of someone in the overlap among several cultures and political and social entities. This was his own experience in growing up as a Mexican-American in the state of Texas. Others prefer the Nahuatl term *nepantla*—the land in between, between two lands. Others describe this experience as one of "exile in our own land," or of an exile from which it is not possible to return. Still others speak about "living in the hyphen"—that is, in the hyphen that both connects and separates the two poles in constructions such as "Mexican-American" or "Cuban-American." All of these images are valuable, and they all point in the same direction. Here, for the sake of both brevity and clarity, I shall focus on the theme of mestizaje.

To be a mestizo is to belong to two realities and at the same time not to belong to either of them. A Mexican-American reared in Texas among people of Euro-American culture is repeatedly told that he is a Mexican—that is, that he does not really belong in Texas. But if that Mexican-American crosses the border hoping to find there his land and his people, he is soon disappointed by being rejected, or at least criticized, as somewhat Americanized—or, as Mexicans would say, for being a *pocho*. Something similar happens to people growing up in New York of Dominican parents and in a Dominican barrio: in the United States they would not be considered fully Americans, and in the Dominican Republic they would be seen as foreigners—or at least as partially foreigners. Such people are both Dominican and North American. At the same time they are neither of the two. And, even though the case of Puerto Rico is somewhat different, there too one has to speak of the mestizaje that is manifest in the very name of the island's status as an *estado libre asociado*—a free associated state. This means that Puerto Rico is free, but not independent. Its colonial status is an "association." Thus Puerto Ricans are American citizens, but if they are asked what their motherland is most would answer Puerto Rico.

Being a mestizo is not only a genetic condition, nor is it limited to one or two generations. There are Mexican-Americans whose ancestors have lived in the United States before the formerly Mexican lands in which they live were taken over by the United States, but they are still Mexican-Americans. There are Cuban-Americans whose Spanish language is rather deficient, and sometimes practically nonexistent, but if someone threatens or denies their Cuban identity, they will immediately come out in its defense.

As Elizondo shows following the insights of Vasconcelos, although often considered inferior, the condition of mestizaje itself is a fertile field for creativity, and quite often it points to the future. In his important book *Galilean Journey*, Elizondo relates all of this—including his own Mexican-American mestizaje—to Galilee in the times of the New Testament. Those from Judea would think they were the true Jews and that Galilee, whose culture and traditions were mixed with traits of Gentile origin, was not truly Jewish. Therefore they called it "Galilee of the Gentiles." But from the point of view of the Romans and other Gentiles, Galileans were Jews. When thus read, the entire story of the Gospels and of the Passion is closely related with Galilean mestizaje and the manner in which the Judeans—Jews from Judea—despised it.

As stated above, and this must always be underscored, the condition of mestizaje is a fertile field for creativity and a sign pointing to the future. To those who claim that "nothing good can come from Nazareth," God responds precisely by offering them a Savior from among those despised people in Galilee. And this is not merely a one-time divine whim, but is the manner in which God repeatedly acts in history and in the church. Most likely not even one line of the New Testament was written in Jerusalem, which was the center of the primitive church. On the contrary, the New Testament was written in what we could well call the mestizaje of the mission to the Gentiles, in that intermediate space in which the early Christians, even though most of them were Jews, were not considered true Jews, while Romans and their authorities did see them as Jews. Western civilization was born of the encounter, conflicts and eventual mestizaje between the Greco-Roman and the Germanic—between that which the ancient Romans called civilization and that which they considered barbaric. The singular creativity of Thomas Aquinas took place in the encounter between Christian medieval Europe and the cultural and philosophical currents that were invading it from the Muslim world.

But that is not all. In speaking of the experience of those who live between two cultures or realities as mestizaje, we have oversimplified reality in order to be able to understand it. Rarely is mestizaje purely bipolar, for quite often the two poles of that mestizaje have within each of them signs of their own mestizaje, thus leading a mestizo to live amid several realities, many of them clashing among themselves. This may be seen in the case of many Latinos and Latinas born in the United States. They are mestizos because they are both Latin Americans and North Americans, and they are frequently told that they are neither one nor the other. But in Latin America most of those Latinos are mestizos in that they carry traits brought from the Iberian Peninsula, which have mixed and still sometimes clash with elements from the various pre-Columbian cultures, and frequently with others of African or Asian origin.

In the case of Augustine, his mestizaje is not simply the encounter between the African and the Roman. Inasmuch as he is an African, he also reflects the mestizo reality of the region, where even before the arrival of the Romans there was a mixture and clash of views and traditions that were Berber or Libyan with others of Punic or Carthaginian origin. And on the Roman side, it is best not to speak of a Roman culture, but rather of a Greco-Roman one, for the *Romanitas* Augustine knew was to a great degree also Greek.

In any case, mestizaje with all its complexities was a constant presence in the life and thought of Augustine as it is also among most of humanity.

For this reason, this book is actually a call to read anew the entire history of the church and its theology from the perspective of mestizaje and of the manner in which it points to the future. And, at least among Christians whose roots are to be found in the western sections of the Roman Empire, among people who spoke Latin, there is no better starting point than Augustine, bishop of Hippo, teacher of generations, and a mestizo.

AUGUSTINE THE MESTIZO

In the pages that follow we shall find ample reason to speak of Augustine as a mestizo, and of his theology as a mestizo theology. But some points may be mentioned as a foretaste. The home in which Augustine was reared, with a Roman father and a mother who was probably of Berber origin, or at least Punic (words that will be explained later on), was clearly mestizo. The same is true of the surrounding atmosphere in Tagaste, the town where Augustine grew up. His first teachers, at the same time that they taught him Roman letters, knew the native language of the area. On the other hand, Augustine worked so hard on his studies of Latin that he was not surpassed in his generation in the use of that language. The form of religion that his mother, Monica, was calling him to accept had clearly African overtones, and this was partly the reason why Augustine, a man versed in Greco-Roman letters and traditions, could not accept it. When the preaching of Ambrose opened for him the path to faith, what he found significant in that preaching was that Ambrose could explain the meaning of that Bible that Monica so loved following the canons of Greco-Roman rhetoric. When he was finally converted, this was partly a conversion to Monica's Christianity and partly a conversion to the "philosophical life" of Neoplatonism. When he faced the Donatists, he found himself having to choose between his African roots and Roman order. Throughout most of his life, it would seem that the Roman in him had become dominant; but when, after the Roman disaster of 410, he tried to read what had happened from a Christian perspective, he was quite critical of the entire Roman culture and civilization, and this criticism was partly grounded on principles learned long before from his Berber mother.

Furthermore, one may even suggest that after Augustine's death the success of his theology was partly due to its being a mestizo theology, one that was not entirely Greco-Roman, when a new mestizaje was being born in Western Europe—the mestizaje between the Roman and the Germanic. Thus Augustine's mestizo theology, now thought to be purely Roman, joined the Germanic cultures in order to create a new mestizaje—a mestizaje that was the cradle of Western civilization and of later theological thought. Let us then turn to Augustine's life, where we shall discover the traits and implications of this mestizaje.

1

A Tortuous Path to Faith

THE CONTEXT

Strange as it may seem, Latin Christian theology did not arise in Rome or even elsewhere in Western Europe, but rather in North Africa. What is more, the first bishop of Rome who wrote in Latin was not a Roman, but an African. Late in the second century Africa was the stage on which Latin theological language developed in the works of Tertullian, who ardently defended his faith both against pagans and against all sorts of heresy. Some decades later that area produced Cyprian, the creator of much of Western ecclesiology and an advocate for the rights of the African episcopacy over against Roman pretensions. And it was in that area that Augustine was born and lived most of his life.

If we find that surprising, we will probably also be surprised to learn that at that time the northern regions of the African continent were not a dry and arid land. At that point the climactic changes that would eventually lead the region to its present condition had not yet taken place. On the contrary, the land in which Augustine was born was rich and fertile. In the areas near the coast, cereals and fruits were produced and cattle were herded. Farther into the interior, on the slopes of mountains, there were abundant olive groves and thick forests. In those forests there were many beasts such as bears and leopards that were hunted and exported to Rome and other cities to serve in the cruel entertainment of those days.

On the other hand, it is important to note that at the time the word *Africa* would not have meant the entire continent that now carries that name. In Augustine's time, that was the name given primarily to the

Roman province of Africa, whose center was the city of Carthage (near where Tunis is today). But, by extension, "Africa" was frequently a way of referring to the northern coast of that continent from Morocco to Libya, but not including Egypt; that is, besides the province of Africa itself, the provinces of Cyrenaica, Numidia, Byzacena, Tripolitania and Mauritania. For the purposes of our history, the region that most interests us is the province of Africa itself and, toward the west, Numidia and Mauritania.

The small town of Tagaste, where Augustine was born in 354 (and which is now called Souk-Ahras), was in Numidia, near the border of the province properly called Africa, or Proconsular Africa. Being in the interior of the land, Tagaste had a population that was mostly Berber, while administration was in Roman hands. Patrick, Augustine's father, was one of the representatives of Roman authority in Tagaste, and therefore he was a person of relative importance within that limited circle, but very secondary within the total framework of the Roman Empire. There were also a few other Roman families in the city. One of them was the family of Alypius, whom Augustine does not seem to have met in Tagaste but somewhat later in Carthage, and whom he called "my soul brother." The very fact that Augustine did not know Alypius until he was in Carthage may be due to the difference in age between them, but more probably to a social scale in Tagaste in which the aristocratic family of Alypius was high above that of Augustine—particularly since Augustine had an African mother. Tagaste was also the hometown of Romanianus, a relatively well-to-do man—and perhaps a distant relative of Patrick and therefore also of Augustine—who saw the promise of young Augustine, opened his library to him and covered the cost of much of his study, apparently hoping that after returning to Tagaste Augustine would become a tutor to his children.

Tagaste would have had a few thousand inhabitants and was the administrative center for the surrounding area, where land was mostly held in latifundia dedicated to cereals, fruit, cattle and olive groves. Most of the owners of such latifundia preferred to live in larger cities such as Carthage or Rome, and therefore the administration of the lands was left in the hands of stewards, some of whom were slaves and some freedmen. As to the population of Tagaste itself, most of it seems to have been of Berber origin, like that of the surrounding area.

Some five or six centuries before the time of Augustine, when Rome was beginning to develop what became its vast empire, the entire area was ruled from Carthage. This was an independent city that had been founded by Phoenician colonizers. In the second century before Christ, it vied with Rome over hegemony over the western Mediterranean. Since these Phoenicians were known as "Punics," the wars between Rome and Carthage are known in history as the "Punic Wars." The struggle was difficult, and at one point the Carthaginian general Hannibal led his troops to the very outskirts of Rome. But in the end Rome won, under the leadership of General Scipio, who was called "the African," not because he came from that land, but rather to honor him as the conqueror of Africa. This was in the year 146 before the birth of Christ, and the Roman senate decreed that Carthage would be demolished so that it would never again rise as a rival to the city set on seven hills. This was done, but less than 120 years later, just before the beginnings of the Christian era, Emperor Augustus ordered that the city be rebuilt, now as part of the Roman Empire and capital of the province of Africa. The success of that new foundation was such that when Augustine was born, less than four centuries later, Carthage was the second largest city in the western Mediterranean, surpassed only by Rome.

But centuries earlier, when those first Punic colonizers reached the area, they did not find it uninhabited but populated by Berbers, or Libyans, a seminomadic people occupying the lands from the Mediterranean coast to the sands of the Sahara. The Berbers did not disappear. Some of them withdrew to more remote areas where Punic power did not reach, while others remained in the conquered lands, subjected to the Punic conquerors. Such Berbers labored in the less respected occupations, did the most arduous work and bore the most onerous taxes.

Thus, in the region that served as the background for most of Augustine's life—the area where he was raised and where he did most of his pastoral and theological work—there were at least three cultural strata, sometimes intermingling and sometimes in conflict. There are indications of many people of Punic or Berber origin seeking to become assimilated within Roman culture and order. But it is also clear that relations between these various groups were not always friendly, and that many resisted the invasions, first by the Punics and later by the Romans. Apparently there was not in the area the strict social stratification that existed, for instance, in Egypt, where a Copt who tried to pass as a Greek or as a Roman was considered a criminal and was punished by the state, and where Greeks and Jews occupied intermediate positions between Copts and Romans. But there was a certain social and economic stratification, so that the higher levels of society were reserved for people of Roman blood, and those who tried to approach such social levels had to abandon their cultural and linguistic traditions, while the rest were called "Berbers" or "Punics." Frequently there was not a clear distinction between these two groups. Therefore, when Augustine speaks of customs, language and traditions as "Punic" it is difficult to know whether he is referring to the ancient Carthaginians of Phoenician origin or to the original inhabitants of the region. Thus, for instance, when he refers to the Punic language it is very possible that he is referring to the most common speech of the area where he was raised, which was actually Berber.

There were three main languages in the area where Augustine was raised: the Latin of the empire and of administration; the Punic language, Semitic in origin, which was rapidly disappearing; and the Libyan language, which the Berbers spoke. The decadence of Punic was such that when Augustine and his contemporaries referred to a language as "Punic" frequently they actually meant Libyan. Augustine himself refers to Libyan as "Punic language, that is, African." As centuries went by, that ancient language of Semitic origin disappeared, and today only echoes of it are heard in the island of Malta, whose language is a combination of ancient Punic with several other languages, and according to some linguists has some traits typical of the Arabic of that area—a language that, as ancient Punic, is also of Semitic origin. As to Libyan, it continued being spoken in the interior of North Africa through the centuries, and it is the background of twenty-first-century Berber—a language that many in the area prefer to Arabic and that, together with Arabic, in this century has become an official language of Morocco, as well as of other regions of North Africa.

As the ancient Punic language was beginning to disappear, in Tagaste and the surrounding areas the most common language was Berber or Libyan. During the twentieth century a series of archaeological diggings have unearthed hundreds of Libyan inscriptions, and some written in both Libyan and Latin; but very few in Punic. Therefore, although there were three languages in North Africa, two of them were dominant: the Libyan spoken by the lower echelons of society and in rural areas, and the Latin of administration and aristocracy.

Furthermore, this stratification was not only social but also geographic. The Latin-speaking population was concentrated in the cities, particularly those along the coast. But, with few exceptions, even in the cities those of Latin roots and speech were the elite that ruled over a mostly Berber population. In the last two centuries, excavations in the cemeteries in the area—including the one in Hippo, where Augustine served as a bishop—have led to the conclusion that Libyan or Berber was the language most commonly spoken. Farther south, Libyans or Berbers were by far the majority of the population and had a certain degree of autonomy—although when that autonomy was stretched too far Roman legions would intervene to remind the population that it was part of the Roman Empire.

The difference in cultures was not limited to social and geographic stratification, but also resulted in differences in the values that each of them considered most important. Greco-Roman culture valued order and rationality above all. For centuries, Greek philosophy had been proud of its rationality, of its refusal to allow itself to be carried away by those passions that hide the truths that only reason may know. For their part, Romans had reason to be proud of their legal system—that is, of the way in which they had learned to apply to the social order the principles of rationality that the Greeks had proposed. For this reason, many in the Greco-Roman world were convinced that Stoicism was the best philosophy. It certainly was the most commonly held by Romans in Augustine's time. This was so because Stoicism insisted on knowing the "natural law" that rules over all things, freeing oneself from the passions that hide or oppose that natural law, and thus leading a reasonable life that is the highest level of fulfillment humans can attain. Over against this, African cultures valued emotions and spontaneity. They certainly had laws, but their purpose was not the good of the society at large, but rather the good of the relatively small nucleus of people tied by familial and similar bonds. Such laws were very important, for without them the social nuclei could dissolve. But they were laws of the group and for the group, and not laws imposed from outside on the basis of a supposedly superior rationality. As a consequence of these cultural contrasts, Romans usually saw Berbers as "barbarians" lacking in civilization, and the Punics as slightly better. And the Africans—both Berbers and Punics—would look at the Romans as imperialists who covered the laws and the order they wished to impose under a varnish of rationality.

All this was reflected in the religious life of the area. Ancient Berbers had been polytheists who worshiped a great variety of deities related to the various forces of nature or to a particular sanctuary. But above all these divine beings there was a supreme and wise God known as "the Ancient"—*Senex*. Punics brought with themselves the gods of the lands of Canaan and Phoenicia, dominated by Baal Hammon—from whose name many Punic names are derived, such as Hannibal and Hasdrubal. The rule of this particular god over all others was such that today many see emerging monotheistic tendencies in Punic religion. At any rate, soon Senex and Baal were joined into one, which resulted in a general religiosity that was common to the entire area. When the Romans arrived, they applied there the religious policy that they followed in their various conquests: while bringing their own gods and promoting their worship, they tolerated the various religions of each place and encouraged a process by which the gods of those religions would become progressively identified with some of the gods of the Roman pantheon. In formerly Punic lands efforts were made to identify Baal Hammon with Saturn. This policy seems to have succeeded, for ancient documents indicate that the population of that region was devoted to Saturn. But scholars who have studied the matter make it clear that the "Saturn" whom Punics worshiped was more like the ancient Baal Hammon than like the Roman Saturn.

Christianity seems to have arrived in North Africa during the second half of the second century, probably from Italy but perhaps from Phrygia. It soon developed deep roots, and, as already stated, African Christianity took the lead in theological production in the Latin language. But while some of the leaders of that nascent church were of Roman origin or at least had been assimilated into Roman culture—as in the cases of Tertullian and Cyprian—soon the new faith expanded among the Punic and Berber population. These were times of persecution, when Roman authorities opposed Christianity, and therefore it seems likely that the conversion to the new religion by many Africans had overtones of a protest against the existing order, or at least a desire to reclaim a truth and authority beyond the truths and authority of the dominant population.

Therefore it is not surprising that there was always in the area a type of Christianity marked by its strong opposition to Greco-Roman culture. We find an echo of that attitude in the writings of Tertullian, whose criticism—and even mockery—of that culture is symptomatic. Toward the end of his life, when it seemed to him that orthodox Christianity was becoming too easily reconciled to the customs and perspectives of the dominant culture, Tertullian and many others opted for Montanism, a movement that was quite critical of the dominant culture and social order. Paradoxically, one of the reasons we know of Tertullian is that he himself appears to be of Latin rootage and certainly was well-versed in Latin law and language, so that his Latin writings were appreciated by the rest of Latin Christendom. But we may well imagine how many other anonymous Christians of Berber or Punic origin held similar opinions and feelings.

A goodly part of the Christian population of the area always retained that attitude of distancing from and even opposition to the dominant culture. A few decades before the birth of Augustine, Emperor Constantine decreed tolerance toward Christians, and eventually both he and his successors declared themselves to be Christians and lent imperial support to the church. Christianity became at first politically and culturally acceptable, then the dominant religion of the empire and finally almost the only religion that was tolerated. Significantly, at a time when senators and other Roman aristocrats were flocking to the baptismal waters, and most of the population was following them, something very different was taking place in Africa. With the theological excuse that some of the bishops recognized by the official church had not stood firm during the persecution that was now ended, a good number of Christians in the provinces of Africa and Numidia abandoned that church. These rebellious Christians, known as Donatists after one of their leaders, Donatus, refused to bend before imperial authority now represented by the official church. As we shall see, as time went by this movement became ever more extreme, eventually leading to violence. But what at present is of interest to us is that Donatism spread mostly among the population of Berber and Punic origin—and that among the most extreme Donatists most were Berber. We shall later deal with Donatism and Augustine's polemics against it.

Tagaste, the town where Augustine was born, was in the province of Numidia but very near the border of the province of Africa. Until shortly before Augustine's birth, most of its population was Donatist, and many of them held to that faith even after the death of Augustine. Furthermore, there were always Donatists in Augustine's own family, and some of them came to hold high positions within that movement.

In any case, all Christianity in that area, Donatist as well orthodox, was characterized by certain emphases. There was an inclination in the Latin West, particularly in Africa, to understand the Christian faith in terms of rules and moral principles. As I have explained in more detail elsewhere (*Christian Thought Revisited: Three Types of Theology*), this Western theology saw God foremost as a lawgiver and judge, sin as an infraction of the law of God, the human condition as similar to a moral debt, baptism as a washing away or forgiving of the guilt of sin and the work of Jesus as a payment of that debt on behalf of the believer. The consequences of such a way of understanding the gospel that eventually became widespread throughout the Western church—Catholic as well as

Protestant—were many. One of the first was the debate regarding the holiness of the church. If God is above all a lawgiver and a judge, and if Christian faith is a matter of morality and obedience, how can a church be a true church of Jesus Christ if it is not pure and holy? Some claimed the church was like Noah's ark, in which a few are saved from the surrounding evil, and therefore there is in it no place for sinners. Others claimed that the church is like a field in which wheat and tares grow together and the task of judging who is one or the other belongs to God, not to Christians. This resulted in a long series of schisms, particularly in the West, for if someone comes to the conclusion that the church is not sufficiently pure, the course to be followed is to abandon it for the sake of a new and "true" church. Naturally, there will soon be those who, even within that "true" church, believe even this is not sufficiently pure and then abandon it in order to create an even holier one. These are the attitudes at the root of Donatism, as well as of the many similar groups that developed out of it.

The other consequence of the type of theology that was dominant in the West was the constant debate about what to do with postbaptismal sins. If at baptism a believer's sins are forgiven, what happens when that believer sins after baptism? How can that believer pay or atone for such sins? Eventually this would lead in Roman Catholicism to the development of its entire penitential system, with its purgatory and its indulgences; and in Protestantism, to constant schisms because there are some who think their church is not sufficiently holy. It was this religion of legalistic and moralizing tendencies that Augustine knew through his mother and the community of faith to which she belonged. Augustine himself, although eventually coming to share some of those perspectives, found himself in the lead to reject and refute some of the consequences of these tendencies, as we shall see when discussing his attitudes toward Pelagianism.

His Family

The family into which Augustine was born and where he was raised had intercultural and mestizo characteristics that were relatively common in the area. His father, Patrick by name, was a Roman official with the rank of decurion, and owner of some land. This means that his responsibilities consisted in collecting taxes, and therefore that he would not be very popular among the population that bore most of the tax burden—that is, the "African" population, as distinct from the "Roman." Although he owned some land and slaves, this did not make him rich, for after being able to study for some time in the near city of Madaura Augustine had to return to Tagaste because his family did not have the necessary funds to support his further studies. According to Augustine himself, Patrick was an irascible man who, although never striking his wife, did make her the subject of verbal abuse—and, as was common at that time, Augustine praises his mother for her submissive spirit as she accepted and overcame the wrath of her husband. As to religion, Patrick followed that of his ancestors—what is today called paganism.

Monica, Augustine's mother, was probably of Berber origin, for her name seems to be derived from the goddess Mon, who was worshiped in a nearby sanctuary. But she herself was a faithful and devout Christian whose religion reflected the form of Christianity that was dominant in the area. She was some twenty years younger than her husband. This was common in Roman society, in which it was customary for males to take concubines until they came to a relatively mature age, when it was time to beget legal heirs. We also know that when Monica married Patrick the couple lived for some time with his mother—which was also common practice—who apparently did not approve of her son's marriage, and constantly criticized Monica and sought ways to make her life more difficult. From this marriage between Patrick and Monica at least three children were born: the eldest, Navigius, of whom little is known; Augustine; and a sister whose name and age are unknown—although later tradition began calling her Perpetua—who, at least toward the end of Augustine's days, led a group of women in monastic life.

Of all these people, the only one to whom Augustine repeatedly refers in his writings is Monica. She was a severe woman who from the day of her marriage devoted herself to praying for the conversion of her husband. She never hid this hope that her husband would change, and this may be one of the reasons why both Patrick and his mother dealt with Monica harshly and even cruelly. Eventually, shortly before his death, Patrick did convert to Christianity.

All this shows that quite probably Augustine himself was a mestizo, which would show in a slightly darker skin than that of pure Romans. He was certainly raised in a mestizo atmosphere, not only in the genetic sense but also culturally. The Greco-Roman culture his father represented had a long history of great achievements, and it was the path toward success in the career of civil service that both of his parents planned for him. In Monica he knew a form of Christianity that had normally seen itself in opposition to the surrounding culture, but that was now beginning to adjust to Roman domination. The town of Tagaste itself had been mostly Donatist until a few years before Augustine was born, and therefore one may imagine that Monica represented that accommodation to Roman dominion that was appearing among some of the more traditional elements of Christianity in the region. Patrick was the presence of Rome. Monica represented the Berber, the African—in Roman terms, "barbarism"—seeking a place within Roman society. Patrick was the reminder of Greco-Roman achievements. Monica represented a faith quite ready to obey God above all, and to subject all to that obedience. Throughout his life Augustine lived between those two poles, sometimes leaning in one direction and sometimes in the other. And that may also be seen in his own theological development.

While Augustine was still a young child, Monica was aware of the extraordinary gifts of her son, and she devoted the rest of her life to turning him into a devout Christian with a successful career. This is why one may see in Monica signs of a social mestizaje that was taking place— a mestizaje in which some among the "Africans" sought to climb within the social Roman ladder, very much as immigrants today who, while insisting in the value of their ancestral cultures, insist also in having their children learn the language of their adopted country and leave aside their own culture, so that they may have a greater chance at social and economic success. Augustine always refers to his mother with great respect and devotion, but in his writings we also see the profile of a domineering mother—perhaps of a woman who, being deprived of any authority in her own home as well as any possibility of determining and shaping her own life, lived vicariously in this son whom she practically persecuted until, shortly before her death, she was able to see converted and baptized. Augustine would eventually describe himself as a spoiled child who would throw temper tantrums, crying and screaming until he got what he wanted, and therefore one may well imagine the tensions that would develop between the spoiled young man and his domineering mother.

HIS STUDIES

With the limited resources that they had, Augustine's parents covered the costs of his education in Tagaste. Augustine himself declares that, although he was also intellectually curious, the games and adventures that he enjoyed with his companions interested him much more than his studies. When he finally reached the limit of what could be learned in Tagaste, he went to continue his studies in the city of Madaura (today M'Daourouch), some twenty-five kilometers away. There he studied with a certain Maximus. Much later Augustine would write to him in defense of that which was "African" and "Punic" over against his own teacher, who insisted on the value of all that was Roman, and therefore remained a pagan—which in itself is proof of the degree to which Christianity had become largely a Punic or African religion in the area. Augustine tells Maximus:

> After all, as an African writing to Africans, for we are both living in Africa, you could not forget yourself to such an extent that you thought that Punic names should be criticized. . . . If you disapproved of that language, deny that many words of wisdom have been committed to memory in Punic books, as is disclosed by very learned men. You should, of course, regret that you were born in the place where the cradle of that tongue is still warm.[1]

This is not only interesting but also significant. At about the same time when Augustine was writing this letter, he also confessed that he had scarce knowledge of the Punic (or Berber) language, and he did not dare

---

[1] *Letter* 17.2. NCP II/1:49.

preach in it—but he did cite "Punic proverbs" in his Latin preaching. This is one more example of the mestizaje that provided the context in which young Augustine grew up. It is not very different from the experience of so many Latinos and Latinas in the United States who, while acknowledging that their education has provided them with a very low level of the knowledge of the Spanish language and preferring to speak in English, if someone criticizes Spanish or traditional Latin cultures, immediately rise to defend that language and those cultures.

Before Augustine was able to complete his studies in Madaura, his family ran out of funds, and the young student, who was then sixteen years old, had to return to Tagaste, where he once again joined his friends in pranks and mischief.

It was at that time that the famous incident of the pears took place. According to Augustine, he and a group of friends stole some pears, not in order to eat them, for they were still green, but for the mere pleasure of doing what they should not. Later Augustine would reflect on that incident and several others of like nature, and would see in them a sign of original sin and of his own corruption.

> Close to our vineyard there was a pear tree laden with fruit. This fruit was not enticing, either in appearance or in flavor. We nasty lads went there to shake down the fruit and carry it off at dead of night, after prolonging our games out of doors until that late hour according to our abominable custom. We took enormous quantities, not to feast on ourselves but perhaps to throw to the pigs; we did eat a few, but that was not our motive: we derived pleasure from the deed simply because it was forbidden.
>
> Look upon my heart, O God, look upon this heart of mine, on which you took pity in its abysmal depths. Enable my heart to tell you now what it was seeking in this action which made me bad for no reason, in which there was no motive for my malice except malice. The malice was loathsome, and I loved it. I was in love with my own ruin, in love with decay: not with the thing for which I was falling into decay but with the decay itself, for I was depraved in soul, and I leapt down from your strong support into destruction, hungering not for some advantage to be gained by the foul deed, but for the foulness of it.[2]

---

[2]*Confessions* 2.4. NCP I/1:67-68.

Finally, thanks to a fairly well-to-do neighbor named Romanianus, who took an interest in the future of this very promising young man, Augustine was able to continue his studies. Romanianus did not feel that what was available in Madaura was sufficient, but rather had Augustine sent to Carthage, the great city in North Africa, which was about 250 kilometers away from Tagaste.

Seeing himself for the first time free from the supervision of his parents, Augustine turned to what he would later call a licentious life. He joined a gang of students who apparently called themselves "the destructors," with whom he shared his housing as well as quite a few mischievous adventures—some of them real, and others invented to impress the rest of the gang. As he would later say, at that time he was "in love with the very idea of love," and he sought to satisfy his desires in any possible way. Although he attended church often, he would do this in order to see whom he could seduce. At the same time, at school he appeared to be an exemplary student, fulfilling all his obligations and standing above his fellow students. Thus he led a double life, on the one hand as a young, promising and faithful student, and on the other as a dissolute and venturesome womanizer. But soon, to the great chagrin of his friends as well as his mother, he established permanent relations with a woman—apparently a freed woman—whom he took as a concubine.

The story of this concubine and her relation to Augustine deserves special attention. In order to understand it, it is necessary to take into account that it was neither unusual nor considered immoral that a young man of good family would take a concubine in a quasi-marital relationship for several years. Romans were much concerned over matters of inheritance, and only legitimate or adopted children were able to inherit. Therefore a young man would take a concubine and live with her, frequently in monogamous fidelity, until he was some thirty or forty years old. Then he would take a legal spouse, not out of his own desire to do so or for love, but simply in order to produce legal heirs. When they were actually married some men would abandon their concubines, and others would retain them. But at any rate, concubinage was a socially acceptable relationship. Apparently Augustine was faithful to his concubine during the eleven years that he lived with her. Although it would seem that they sought not to produce offspring, from this union a son was born, whom they named Adeodatus—that is, given by God. The significance of this name is debatable, because even though its actual form is Latin, it is not a typical Latin name, but rather an exact translation of a fairly common Punic name—Iantan-Baal.

Patrick was converted at about that time, and died shortly thereafter. Free from the bonds of her husband, who had forced her to remain in Tagaste, Monica was now able to devote the rest of her days to lead her son along what she considered to be the correct path. She soon appeared in Carthage, where she repeatedly expressed her disgust with the concubine Augustine had taken, and began to encourage him to abandon her. Although there is no doubt that part of her intention was moral, apparently there were other reasons for opposition to Augustine's concubine. When it came to matters of morality, concubinage was not always rejected by the church, for there were many cases in which Christian couples had reasons preventing them or making it inadvisable for them to marry before the law. Therefore the bishops in Africa had declared that a monogamous concubinage, even though not reaching the level of a legal marriage, was acceptable, and Christians living in such a relationship would not be excommunicated as sinful. Perhaps Monica feared that Augustine's permanent relationship with this concubine—apparently a freed woman of African rootage and therefore of inferior social level—would lead to marriage, and this might be an obstacle in the career she planned for her son. Perhaps she feared her son would make the same social error that her own husband had committed in marrying her. So we may well imagine that her relations with her son's concubine were similar to those she had experienced with her own mother-in-law.

Since Augustine was responsible for the expenses of the home he had established with his concubine, he found himself needing to work for their support. With that purpose he returned to Tagaste, where he lived for about a year. By that time he was attracted to Manichaeism—to which we shall soon return—and Monica, who had returned earlier, refused to receive him. Eventually, apparently with much reluctance, she was reconciled with this son of hers who was being led astray by heresy. But in Tagaste things did not go well. Augustine's finances were precarious, his relations with Monica were tense and his best friend died unexpectedly. Disgusted and pained by all this, Augustine decided to return to Carthage with his concubine and Adeodatus.

Since his studies had centered on rhetoric, for eight years Augustine taught that subject in Carthage and was able to collect enough students to cover his expenses. But this would not satisfy him, partly because he was becoming increasingly convinced that rhetoric itself was a discipline void of content, and partly because his students paid little attention to him and followed the same sort of dissolute lifestyle that he had followed earlier. At that point he sought to make his way in the field of literature, and he wrote his first book. But nobody bought it or paid any attention to it. Finally, disgusted by his life in Carthage, he decided to go to Rome, once again taking with him Adeodatus and his concubine. Monica was opposed to that project, partly because she did not want her son so far away from her, and partly because she feared the pagan influences in the imperial capital. Finally Augustine escaped, telling his mother that he had decided to stay in Carthage and taking a ship that very night, fleeing with the ebbing tide.

During those years that he had spent in Carthage, while he continued his studies and his own teaching and sought a means to support his family, his restless mind had led Augustine along unexpected routes. Rhetoric was not concerned about whether something was true or not, but only about the best way to convince an audience by means of elegant speech and persuasive argument. One of the great orators of Roman antiquity was Marcus Tullius Cicero, and therefore Augustine began studying his writings earnestly—particularly the *Hortensius*. But Cicero had also been a philosopher, and soon Augustine was convinced that it was not enough to speak well, but it was also necessary to seek after truth. Later Augustine declared,

> My interest in the book was not aroused by its usefulness in the honing of my verbal skills (which was supposed to be the object of the studies I was

now pursuing, in my nineteenth year, at my mother's expense, since my father had died two years earlier): no, it was not merely as an instrument for sharpening my tongue that I used that book, for it had won me over not by its style but by what it had to say.[3]

Thus began a long intellectual pilgrimage that led first to Stoicism after the manner of Cicero, then during a short time to skepticism, then to Manichaeism and eventually back to the Christian faith of his mother.

Stoicism was an eminently practical philosophy, for it was not so much concerned about abstract truth as about the manner of living life wisely. What was important was not to understand things, but rather to understand life. Thus it was necessary to know "the law of nature," and to live according to that law, for it is in so doing that happiness is to be found. Happiness is not in attaining what one desires, but rather in desiring what one ought. One who is truly wise is not carried away by passion, but rather reaches "apathy"—which literally means the lack of passions—and leads a rational life. Augustine decided that although all of this was true it was not enough. The teachings of his mother and the biblical stories he had heard in the cradle spoke of a truth far beyond all of this, a truth that would explain the origin and purpose not only of life but also of the entire universe. Furthermore, if the main requirement of a wise life was to overcome passion, Augustine knew that he was incapable of doing so, for even in spite of his best intentions passions led him where his reason told him he should not go.

Remembering Monica's teachings, Augustine went to Scripture in search of that great truth that he needed. But after his studies of rhetoric he found the stories and the style of the Christian Scriptures wanting. As a rhetorician, he felt that these Scriptures were not worthy of comparison with the majestic writings of Cicero. Augustine knew neither Hebrew nor Greek (although he had studied the latter language, he never liked it, and therefore never learned it well), and he therefore read Scripture in an ancient Latin version of unknown origin, the *Vetus Latina*. This was not always a felicitous translation, and it was a few years later, while Augustine

---

[3]*Confessions* 3.4. NCP I/1:79.

was still alive, that Jerome produced the Vulgate, an excellent translation that was soon generally accepted. Therefore the Latin Bible that Augustine read was not as elegant as the Vulgate. But what concerned him was not only the lack of stylistic elegance in the use of Latin but also that the stories themselves he found in the Bible, with its wars, rebellions, exiles and all the rest, did not seem to have much to say to someone who was in quest of truth.

MANICHAEISM

It was then that he began to be interested in Manichaeism. This was a religion born in Persia that seemed to explain the origin and workings of the world on the basis of a radical dualism. According to the Manichaeans, there are two eternal and indestructible principles: the principle of light and the principle of darkness. These two should always have been separated; but in the present world the two are intermingled, and this is the reason for evil. As for the human being, this too is an admixture of darkness (the body) and light (the soul). Salvation then consists in separating the soul from the body, since only the soul can be saved, while the body is an obstacle on the way to the soul's liberation and will eventually return to the reign of darkness. All of this seemed to solve one of the greatest difficulties Augustine found in Christian doctrine: If there is only one God, and if God is good, how does one explain the existence of evil?

Augustine joined the Manichaeans. Although he was a member of their sect for many years, he never went beyond being a "hearer" to become one of the "elect." Apparently he never felt toward his own body the horror the "perfect" felt toward theirs. Some of them so despised their own body that through a ritual practice called *endura* they would fast until they died as a result. Furthermore, although Manichaeism seemed to solve Augustine's difficulties with the origin of evil, there were still many unanswered questions. When Augustine posed such questions to the Manichaean leaders, he was told that soon Faustus, the great Manichaean teacher, would come to Carthage and would clear all his doubts. But when the much announced Faustus arrived, Augustine did not find in him any greater wisdom than in those other Manichaeans who had been unable to answer his questions. Showing the distrust of mere rhetoric that had earlier been fostered by reading Cicero, Augustine commented:

> When he came, then, he did indeed impress me as a man of pleasant and smooth speech, who chattered on the usual themes much more beguilingly than the rest. A man adept at serving fine wines, then; but what was that to me in my thirst? My ears were sated with such offerings already. The content did not seem better to me for being better presented, nor true because skillfully expressed, nor the man wise of soul because he had a handsome face and a graceful turn of speech. Those who had held out promises to me were not good judges; to them he seemed wise and prudent merely because they enjoyed the way he talked.[4]

From that point on, although Augustine still continued relating to the Manichaeans, he was dissatisfied with this religion that momentarily had seemed an answer to his doubts.

---

[4]*Confessions* 5.10. NCP I/1:119-20.

2

Conversion and Baptism

MILAN

In the previous chapter we left Augustine as he fled with his concubine and child to Rome, sneaking away from his mother, disenchanted with Manichaeism and still in an anguishing quest for truth. His first months in Rome were rather difficult, for he lacked both money and employment, and he and his family were able to subsist only thanks to the support of the Manichaeans with whom he gathered. He also became seriously ill, to the point that his survival seemed to be in doubt. But little by little he became known, and he began to gather a group of students of rhetoric that produced sufficient income to be able to subsist. Finally, a year after Augustine had arrived in Rome, his friend Simacus, who was a Manichaean and also a prefect of the city, recommended him for an opening in Milan, which was then one of the cities of imperial residence, and where his career as a professor of rhetoric finally began showing some promise. Since Augustine now prospered economically, there soon gathered around him—and at his expense—a small circle including several friends; his mother, Monica; his brother, Navigius; his concubine; Adeodatus; and other relatives.

Upon arriving in Milan, Augustine had already set aside most of his earlier Manichaean notions, and it would seem that while he still related to the Manichaeans in that city, this was mostly a matter of social relationships rather than of a common belief. His disappointment upon hearing the famous Faustus led him for a brief time to skepticism—the skepticism of those who called themselves "academics," and against which he would later write. But skepticism seemed to him a facile capitulation in his quest for truth, and he soon abandoned it. Meanwhile, Monica kept insisting he should return to the faith in which she had brought him up.

NEOPLATONISM

In the midst of all these emotional and intellectual struggles, Augustine began turning toward the teachings of the Neoplatonists. Some time earlier, in the work of Plotinus and others, ancient Platonism had become a religious philosophy. According to this doctrine, all reality proceeds from the One in a series of emanations or concentric circles, so that the more distant they are from that One, moving toward multiplicity, they are less valuable and less good. This One is purely spiritual, for in the hierarchy of being matter stands far below that which is incorporeal and spiritual.

As Augustine would later attest, Neoplatonism helped him find solutions to two issues that had always stood in the way to accepting Christian doctrine: the matter of how to explain the existence of evil, and how God can exist without a body.

As to the existence of evil, in contrast with the Manichaeans the Neoplatonists held that there is no such thing as a principle of evil. Reality is not twofold, as the Manichaeans held, but is rather an emanation from that single source that is the One. Evil then is simply a distancing from that One. That which most approaches it is best, and that which departs from it and inclines to multiplicity is worse. There is no reality that in itself is evil. Everything is good. Something is said to be bad when it does not occupy its proper place in the hierarchy of being. Among the many examples that Augustine offers, one is a monkey. The monkey itself is not ugly. As a monkey, it is beautiful and is what it ought to be. But if a human being takes the shape of a monkey, one says this is ugly, that it is not what it ought to be, that something is wrong. Likewise, intellectual beings—souls and angels—have been created for the contemplation of the One, and if they forsake that contemplation and lean toward the multiple, that is evil. So, rather than the dualism of Manichaeism, which for a time seemed to explain the existence of evil, Augustine now opted for Neoplatonic monism, and this helped him understand that it is possible that there be evil in a world created by a God who is good. "I inquired then what villainy might be, but I found no substance, only the perversity of a will twisted away from you, God, the supreme substance, toward the depths."[1]

Neoplatonism also helped Augustine to understand the existence of a purely spiritual God such as that of Monica's Christianity. The Stoic philosophy Augustine had learned from Cicero and others, as well as several other philosophies then circulating in the Greco-Roman world, held that all reality is corporeal. The soul, the gods and any other spiritual being that may be conceived are only more subtle bodies than these our eyes see. The Epicureans, diametrically opposed to Stoicism on many points, agreed that the intellect is nothing but a body composed of atoms that are smaller than those of the physical body. In opposition to such views Monica and Christians in general held that there is a purely spiritual God—which from the point of view of both Stoicism and Epicureanism would seem to be nonsense. But now Augustine found in the teachings of the Neoplatonists the claim that there is in fact a spiritual reality—furthermore that in the last analysis all reality is spiritual, and matter is merely a distancing from the ultimate reality, the One.

Thus Neoplatonism helped Augustine to overcome two of the main intellectual obstacles that stood in the way of his accepting Monica's faith. However, it also led him to a monism in which the world is merely an emanation of the ineffable One and not a creation of the divine will. Later he would leave such monism aside, but would continue explaining the nature of evil as he had learned from Neoplatonism.

AMBROSE

Augustine still felt that the Scriptures Monica claimed to be the Word of God were lacking in literary or philosophical value. In Milan, he heard about the great oratorical gifts of Ambrose, the bishop of the city,

---

[1] *Confessions* 7.16.22. NCP I/1:176.

so he decided to go listen to him, seeking to learn not what he said but how he said it.

> With professional interest I listened to him conducting disputes before the people, but my intention was not the right one: I was assessing his eloquence to see whether it matched its reputation. I wished to ascertain whether the readiness of speech with which rumor credited him was really there, or something more, or less. I hung keenly upon his words, but cared little for their content, and indeed despised it, as I stood there delighting in the sweetness of his discourse.[2]

But Ambrose surprised him not so much by how he spoke, but rather by what he said.

> Nonetheless as his words, which I enjoyed, penetrated my mind, the substance, which I had overlooked, seeped in with them, for I could not separate the two. As I opened my heart to appreciate how skillfully he spoke, the recognition that he was speaking the truth crept in at the same time, though only by slow degrees. At first the case he was making began to seem defensible to me, and I realized that the Catholic faith, in support of which I had believed nothing could be advanced against the Manichean opponents, was in fact intellectually respectable. This realization was particularly keen when once, and again, and indeed frequently, I heard some difficult passage of the Old Testament explained figuratively; such passages had been death to me because I was taking them literally.[3]

These words show how upon listening to Ambrose Augustine was able to join the Roman culture of his father to his mother's faith. At this stage in his life, he did this through the allegorical interpretation of Scripture. By such interpretation, Ambrose could overcome the difficulties about Scripture that most bothered Augustine. Such allegorical interpretation, today rightly criticized, at that time was a perfectly acceptable rhetorical device. Augustine himself employed it as he analyzed classical literature and explained it to his students. It was now clear to him that these various biblical passages that before he took to be

---

[2]*Confessions* 5.13.23. NCP I/1:131.
[3]*Confessions* 5.14.24. NCP I/1:132.

absurd or uncouth actually had profound contents. They pointed to eternal truths. They combined the Stoic call to a wise life with the Neoplatonic proclamation of the ineffable One.

From that point on, thanks in part to Neoplatonism and in part to Ambrose and other interpreters who saw in Scripture a more profound and spiritual sense, Augustine was able to accept his mother's faith, at least intellectually. He now had no real reason to doubt that faith nor to think that it was incompatible with the best of Greco-Roman culture.

INTERNAL STRUGGLES

But this did not resolve other issues with which Augustine was struggling. The teacher of rhetoric who was seeking after philosophical truth was also enmeshed in difficult personal decisions. Monica insisted that he must abandon his concubine. He resisted. He finally did so, sending her back to Carthage and keeping Adeodatus with him. It was a cruel decision, and Augustine has frequently been criticized because he does not even mention the name of that woman who had given him so many years of her life. Others argue that quite possibly he did not mention her name because when he wrote his *Confessions* she was probably living in the nearby city of Carthage, and to give that name in a book that he intended to publish would have been a grave indiscretion that would probably cause her even greater distress. Whatever the case may be, the fact is that Augustine was not too pleased with having to break away from her. On the contrary, he would still remember the pain of that separation that was forced on him by his mother.

> The woman with whom I had been cohabiting was ripped from my side, being regarded as an obstacle to my marriage. So deeply was she engrafted into my heart that I was left torn and wounded and trailing blood.[4]

But his surrender to Monica's pressure did not lead Augustine to a purer life. Monica immediately made arrangements so that her son would marry a young girl of good family, hoping that this marriage would help him in his civil career. But the girl was still too young, and

---

[4]*Confessions* 6.15.25. NCP I/1:156.

the promised marriage had to be delayed. Meanwhile, deprived of his concubine of many years, Augustine sought release in other women, and soon took a new concubine—if not with the explicit support of Monica, apparently at least with her tacit agreement.

On top of all this there were also issues of health that threatened Augustine's professional career. He began suffering with what some today think was an asthma of psychosomatic origin—the result of his anxieties and his pain. As he himself tells the story:

> It happened by coincidence that in that same summer my lungs had begun to fail under the severe strain of teaching, making it difficult for me to draw breath and giving proof of their unhealthy condition by pains in my chest. My tone was husky and I could not manage any sustained vocal effort. These symptoms had worried me when they first appeared, because they were forcing upon me the necessity of either giving up my professional career or, if there were any prospect of my being cured and recovering my strength, at least of taking some rest.[5]

All of this placed the young professor of rhetoric amid a flood of emotions, convictions, resolutions soon forsaken, the wish to live the faith of his mother and the strong inclination to reject that faith that seemed so rigid and impracticable. As he himself would later say, at that point his prayer to God was: "Give me chastity, but not just yet."[6]

What made this flood of contradictions even more anguishing was partly that very Neoplatonism that had earlier helped Augustine to overcome his intellectual doubts and that now led him to think that were he to accept Monica's faith he would have to follow the path of what was then called the "philosophical life" or, among Christians of similar inclinations, the life of "Christian leisure"—that is to say, a life of contemplation, study, prayer and sexual abstinence. Shortly thereafter Augustine would declare:

> I could think of no better dream than to be able to devote myself completely to the study of wisdom, nor did I see the possibility of a happy life

---

[5]*Confessions* 9.2.4. NCP I/1:211.
[6]*Confessions* 8.7.17. Unless otherwise indicated, translations from Augustine are the author's.

without being conformed to that wisdom. But I found myself tied by the urgency of tending to my work and those whom I had to support, as well as by many other needs. I also was concerned that my actions might lead my relatives to a life of shame.[7]

Apparently Monica did not understand things in the same way, for at the same time that she was hoping her son would embrace that faith, she was taking steps so that he would marry in such a way that this would enhance his social status. And Augustine himself was afraid that if he had declared publicly that he had become a Christian, many of the better-educated and most respected people in the city would think he had joined a religion that was beneath him.

THE GARDEN

So things stood when Augustine met "a certain Pontianus," who happened to be an African like himself. Upon seeing Augustine reading the letters of Paul, Pontianus began telling him about the heroes of Christianity, particularly about the monks who had withdrawn to the Egyptian desert and those who lived just outside the city of Milan. Augustine was surprised that there were still people who devoted their lives to the Christian faith with such commitment, and was ashamed of not being able to do likewise. That shame overwhelmed him when he learned of the conversion of Marius Victorinus. Victorinus had translated into Latin many of the Neoplatonic writings that Augustine so admired. But now Victorinus himself had been converted to Christianity and, even though he was offered the opportunity to embrace his new faith in private and thus to avoid the ridicule of many of his colleagues, he had insisted on doing it publicly, as the most humble and simple of believers. Up to that point Augustine was able to imagine that the faith of the desert monks was best suited for simple and unlettered people, and not for the highly educated such as himself. Perhaps one could say that it was a faith suited for such Berbers as his mother, but not for those who really knew the beauties and wisdom of Greco-Roman knowledge and literature. But

---

[7] *Against the Academicians* 2.2.4.

now one of his own heroes in the knowledge of that classical culture had openly declared himself to be Christian. This was too much for Augustine, who described his struggles quite dramatically.

> Within the house of my spirit the violent conflict raged on, the quarrel with my soul that I had so powerfully provoked in our secret dwelling, my heart, and at the height of it I rushed to Alypius with my mental anguish upon my face. "What is happening to us?" I exclaimed. "What does this mean? What do you make of it? The untaught are rising up and taking heaven by storm, while we with all our dispassionate teachings are still groveling in this world of flesh and blood! Are we ashamed to follow, just because they have taken the lead, yet not ashamed of lacking the courage even to follow?"[8]

It was then, in that garden in Milan, that the famous incident took place that is usually called "the conversion of Augustine." He tells us that he was crying bitter tears in view of his inability to follow the path that he had discovered should be his when he heard the voice of a child repeating: *tolle lege, tolle lege*—take and read, take and read. He ran back to a place where he had left a book of Paul's epistles.

> I snatched it up, opened it and read in silence the passage on which my eyes first lighted: *Not in dissipation and drunkenness, nor in debauchery and lewdness, nor in arguing and jealousy; but put on the Lord Jesus Christ, and make no provision for the flesh or the gratification of your desires.* I had no wish to read further, nor was there need. No sooner had I reached the end of the verse than the light of certainty flooded my heart and all dark shades of doubt fled away.[9]

CASSICIACUM

The experience in the garden in Milan led Augustine to embark on the life of "Christian leisure" that had been his ideal but that he had not dared embrace. He retired to the country home of his friend Verecundus in Cassiciacum, at the foot of the Alps, together with Monica, Adeodatus

---

[8]*Confessions* 8.8.19. NCP II/1:199.
[9]*Confessions* 8.12.26. NCP I/1:207.

and four other friends—including Alypius, his closest friend, who later became bishop of Tagaste. This was the fall of 386, and Augustine would not return to Milan until the following spring. Apparently, Monica managed the place, and Augustine and the others devoted themselves to study, meditation, and philosophical and religious conversation. It was there in Cassiciacum, after his experience in the garden and before his baptism, that Augustine wrote his earliest surviving works. They show what were the themes that were most engaging to him at the time; and also that, while he was dealing with profound religious questions, he was not particularly interested in the church as such, or in its mission within society. They were works reflecting that "Christian leisure" which was dedicated to the spiritual pleasure of considering religion and philosophy in the exclusive company of a small group of friends with similar interests.

The first literary product of this life of supposed leisure was his treatise *Against the Academicians*, a work in three books that he composed in less than three days in the month of November. He addressed it to his previous benefactor Romanianus, thanks to whom he had been able to study and who now found himself in difficult circumstances. Augustine was trying to make sure that Romanianus would not think that the money invested in Augustine's studies had been a waste, and also wished to show his benefactor that the goods and pomp of the world, rather than leading to happiness, could hinder the way to it. In a call to the "philosophical life" in which he also invites Romanianus to follow it and explains to him why he has abandoned his career as a professor of rhetoric, Augustine tells him:

> That trait, that disposition of yours that has always led you to seek honesty and beauty, and which has made you to be more liberal than rich, by which you preferred to be just rather than powerful, without ever yielding to adversity or injustice, that was I know not what divine gift in you. This was buried in the lethargic dream of your life. But now the hidden providence of God has decided to awaken it with these various and shattering events.
>
> I beg you, awake! Awake! Believe me this will lead you to a joy you have not experienced with the fame and favors of this world by which the heedless are seduced. They also tried to seduce me, even though I thought

daily about these things, until I was forced by a severe heartache to abandon my professional quackery and take refuge in the bosom of philosophy.[10]

The argument of this entire work is that a wise life is possible precisely because it is possible to attain wisdom. According to the "academicians"— that is, the skeptics—it is impossible to find truth. But it is not so, for we at least know what we feel. As Augustine says, "I cannot see how an academician can refute someone who says: 'I know that this seems white to me,' or 'I know that this is a pleasure to my ears.'"[11] Therefore Augustine invites Romanianus to follow the path of the Platonists, but always under the guidance of divine revelation.

> It is quite clear that we are impelled into learning by two forces: authority and reason. And I am quite convinced that I must not set aside the authority of Christ, for I know of no other that is as firm. Since I am such that I am constantly seeking after further truth, not only through faith, but also by understanding, when I delve into subjects requiring difficult reasoning I expect to find among the Platonists the doctrine that best conforms with our revelation.[12]

It was at about the same time that he also wrote *On Order*, in two books, where he deals with the problem of the existence of evil—the very problem that had perplexed him to the point of leading him to seek truth in Manichaean dualism. This book, written in an elegant style reminiscent of the dialogues of Plato, records a series of conversations on the order of the universe and how it reflects the purposes and governance of divine providence. Monica was a participant in some of these conversations, and Augustine says that in them "I came to see her spirit to such a point that it seemed to me that no one was as able as she for the cultivation of true philosophy."[13] In this work he returns to the subject of the path to knowledge, which he had already tackled in *Against the Academicians*, and once again he holds to the opinion of the Platonists, that only the few who are truly wise can attain to truth, while "the many"—*hoi polloi*—must be

---

[10]*Against the Academicians*, intro. 1.3.
[11]*Against the Academicians* 3.20.43.
[12]*Against the Academicians* 3.20.43.
[13]*On Order* 2.1.1.

content with accepting the truth that the wise affirm: "There are two paths that lead to knowledge: authority and reason. Authority is first in the order of time, but reason is actually preferable. . . . Thus, although to the ignorant multitude it seems that the authority of the good is to be preferred, the wise actually prefer reason."[14]

Augustine's argument is essentially what he had learned from the Neoplatonists. From that perspective, evil does not exist as a substance, but is rather a distancing from the good, which in truth is all that exists. This leads him to the point of affirming that even moral evil has its place in the order of providence. Licentius, one of his conversation partners, asks him "if all that the fool does he also does within the order of providence." Licentius himself answers his question by declaring that "although the fluttering life of fools is not ordered by themselves, even so divine providence places it within its order."[15] Augustine then intervenes in the conversation, affirming what Licentius has said through a series of similes: the executioner has a place in society, as do also prostitutes and other people of immoral behavior. What one sees then in the social order, as well as in the animal realm, according to other examples that Augustine offers, is that divine providence places everything in its proper place. Later, particularly as he was writing against the Manichaeans, he felt it necessary to make more room for free will as the reason and origin of moral evil, so that it would be impossible to justify such evil by claiming that it is simply part of the total order of the universe.

Also at a later date Augustine would criticize what he wrote in this book for having given Plato too much credit and not taking sufficient account of the differences between the doctrines of Plato and those of the gospel. Thus in his *Retractations* or *Revisions* (year 426) he would contrast Plato's concept of the world of ideas with the Christian hope of a world to come.

> I regret that in these books . . . I spoke of two worlds, one sensible and the other intelligible, as though the Lord had wanted to signify such a thing

---

[14]*On Order* 2.9.26.
[15]*On Order* 2.3.8.

because he did not say, "My kingdom is not of the world," but rather, *My kingdom is not of this world.* . . . If, to be sure, some other world was being signified by the Lord Christ, it could more easily have been understood in the passage where [it is said that] there will be *a new heaven and a new earth.* . . . When what we pray for when we say *thy kingdom come* . . . will be achieved.[16]

It was also in that November that he wrote *On the Happy Life* or *De beata vita*, a short treatise set in a series of conversations spurred by his birthday (November 13). There, employing the allegory of the anxieties of a sea voyage, he provides a glimpse of what would later become his great spiritual autobiography, the *Confessions*. He also describes what he understands by the "philosophical life," the "happy life" or "Christian leisure," which he believes to be the ideal life. In doing so he employs ideas and phrases drawn from the philosophy of his time, particularly from Cicero. It is interesting to note that in this particular work Monica has the last word: "This is without any doubt the happy life, for it is the perfect life, . . . to which we may be guided in the wings of a firm faith, a joyful hope, and a burning love."[17]

Finally, among the writings produced in those tranquil days in Cassiciacum, one must mention the *Soliloquies*, written that winter immediately after the other writings. Following the model of Seneca, who had composed a dialogue between reason and the senses, Augustine writes a series of inner dialogues between himself and his own reason. It is a most valuable book, in which one finds prayers such as this:

> God, Creator of all things, give me first of all the grace to pray to you properly; then make me worthy of being heard; and, finally, deliver me. . . . God, to withdraw from You is to fall. To turn to You is to rise up. To remain in You is to be firm. God, to depart from You is to die. To return to You is to be revived. To dwell in You is to live. God, whom no one loses except by deceit, whom no one seeks except by being called, and whom no one finds except by being purified.[18]

---

[16]*Revisions* 1.3.2. NCP I/2:31-32.
[17]*De beata vita* 4.35.
[18]*Soliloquies* 1.1.2-3.

The central theme of the *Soliloquies* is the knowledge of truth, which Augustine summarizes as "the knowledge of God and of the soul"—which reminds us of the manner in which many centuries later John Calvin would describe the basic program of human knowledge. Augustine was so passionate about this knowledge that he even declares that his friends are only a means for him to attain to truth, and that "I love wisdom for itself, and the only reason why we should wish to possess anything else or fear their lack is truth itself. This includes life, rest, and friends."[19]

The truth that Augustine sought is to be understood in Platonic terms, as knowledge of that which is absolutely immutable and purely rational. Therefore that quest requires "a radical flight from all things sensible."[20] From that perspective "only immortal things are true,"[21] and "one does not err by looking at deceitful appearances but rather by agreeing to them."[22] It is also his Platonism that leads Augustine to statements that would seem to indicate that at that time he still was considering the possibility of the preexistence of souls[23] (although he later retracted this), and that he agreed with the Platonists that error is a sort of forgetfulness: "You are not to fear your death, but rather forgetting that you are immortal."[24] Platonism also leads him to suggest a manner of proving the truth of his own existence that reminds us of the *Discourse on Method* of Descartes.

> Reason: You who wish to know yourself, do you know that you exist?
> Augustine: I do.
> Reason: How so?
> Augustine: I do not know.
> Reason: Do you know that you think?
> Augustine: I do.
> Reason: Therefore that it is true that you think.
> Augustine: Certainly.[25]

---

[19]*Soliloquies* 1.12.20; 1.13.22.
[20]*Soliloquies* 1.14.24.
[21]*Soliloquies* 1.15.29.
[22]*Soliloquies* 2.3.3.
[23]*Soliloquies* 2.20.
[24]*Soliloquies* 2.19.33.
[25]*Soliloquies* 2.1.1.

In all of this we see the Augustine of Greco-Roman culture, imitator of Seneca and Cicero and—even though he never learned Greek well—of Plato and Plotinus. His ideal is the idle life of the philosopher devoted to the consideration of profound subjects and to conversation about them with other persons of similar inclinations. There is nothing here about the community of the church as the setting for Christian life. There is an affirmation of the authority of revelation and of the gospel, but that authority seems to be disconnected from the church. And little is said about the place of worship—although there is much about prayer in the midst of the select group gathered in Cassiciacum. There is also little about the practice of charity toward the needy as an essential element of faith, or about the mission of the church and of believers.

But all of this is only one of the two main facets of Augustine's faith. His mother, who was able to participate in the conversations of Cassiciacum even though she had not pursued studies such as those of Augustine and his companions, would always remind him that there is a community of faith beyond the limits of the "life of leisure" of a Christian philosopher. In a letter that has unfortunately been lost, Augustine had written to Ambrose telling him of his errors and doubts, and asking him to indicate some readings that would be of help to him. Ambrose recommended that he read the prophet Isaiah; Augustine began reading that book, and he found it so difficult to understand that he postponed its reading for a time when his faith would be more advanced.

Augustine knew, because Monica had always taught this to him, that participation in the community of faith is essential for Christian life, and that an individual believer joins that community by means of baptism. It was not enough to inquire about God and the soul. In order to accept Monica's faith it was also necessary to accept her church, and to do this through a public confession of faith—as had been done earlier by his very admired Marius Victorinus. Therefore, after a few months in Cassiciacum, Augustine returned to Milan to be baptized.

His Baptism

Back in Milan, Augustine was registered among candidates for baptism, together with his son, Adeodatus, and his best friend, Alypius. It was already March, and Augustine hoped to be baptized on Easter Eve, that is, on the night between the 24th and 25th of April of that very year, 387. A century earlier such a thing would not have been allowed, for normally the catechumenate—the period of formal preparation for baptism— would last at least two years. But now things had changed. As the empire declared itself Christian under Constantine and his successors, the church was flooded by candidates asking for baptism, and did not have the necessary number of teachers to continue the rigorous program of catechumenate that had existed before. Therefore the process was shortened. Ambrose, who would baptize Augustine, had been elected bishop of Milan when he was still not even baptized, and within a week the necessary steps were taken so that he could move all the way from being a catechumen to being a bishop. But even so, requesting baptism and receiving it the following month was still uncommon. What happened in Augustine's case was the application of a procedure that he himself would suggest thirteen years later in his treatise *On the Instruction of the Unlearned.*

That treatise was written in 400 CE, when Deogratias, a deacon in Carthage who was very much sought after as an instructor of catechumens, wrote Augustine asking for his advice as to how best to perform his task. In his response, Augustine offers an outline of what is to be taught and how. But he also offers an exception that is a reference to his own case.

> We are not to forget the case of those who come to you in order to be catechized, but have already been instructed in liberal arts and have decided to become Christians, so that they now come to you seeking to be able to receive the sacraments. It is quite likely that such people, from a long time before becoming Christians, have mulled profoundly on these matters, and have discussed and conversed with all that they could about their own feelings. You are to deal with those people briefly, not tediously teaching them what they already know, but humbly mentioning it, so that

they can tell you that they already know this or that without having it hammered into them, as in the case of the unlearned or ignorant. . . . It is also advisable for you to ask them why they wish to become Christians, and what books they have read, both in Scripture and by good commentators. . . . All of these matters are to be discussed humbly with those who come to the Christian community not as unlearned, but rather having already been polished and cultivated through the books of the learned.[26]

Since Augustine and his companions were precisely the sort of people whom he was describing in these words, they were baptized after a brief instruction of a few weeks. But this does not mean that for them baptism was not very significant. The preparation given to them before they would be allowed to receive that sacrament would be of great importance. For several weeks, Augustine and his companions received instruction on the Christian faith and the teachings of the church—even though at that point still some of these teachings would be considered so holy as not to be given until the very last moment.

Finally, on April 24, on the eve of Easter, the entire church gathered in the basilica where Ambrose was leading worship. Neither Augustine nor his companions nor any other of the candidates for baptism were there. They had gathered in another area near the basilica, the baptistery. There the men were separated from the women, for they were to be baptized naked. Before being baptized, each of them had to issue a formal renunciation of the devil and the world with all its pomp, probably turning toward the west, a symbol of darkness, and spitting in a sign of disgust. Then they would turn to the east and declare their faith in Jesus Christ, the Sun of Justice.

Like the others, Augustine entered the baptismal waters where he knelt while Ambrose inquired about his faith in the Father, the Son and the Holy Spirit, and poured water over his head three times. After coming out of the waters, each received a white tunic—not as a sign of purity, but rather of newness of life and of victory, for at that time the color white was a symbol of victory. Then they were anointed with oil, indicating that

---

[26]*On the Instruction of the Unlearned* 1.8.12-13.

now they were kings and priests, part of the "royal priesthood" that is the people of God.

Still clad in their white tunics, the neophytes then entered the basilica, where the congregation received them with acclamation. If, as is most likely, the ancient rites of former centuries were still practiced, they would be given to drink, besides the chalice of wine, another of water as a sign of their inner baptism, and a third one of milk and honey, proclaiming their entrance into the Promised Land. At any rate, it was there that for the first time Augustine received that Communion of which his mother had been partaking for several decades at least once a week, and therefore he now became part of the same body of Christ of which his mother was a member.

Although Augustine was baptized by Ambrose, apparently the latter was not aware of the promise of this neophyte, for in his own writings he does not mention that he baptized Augustine. But the joint presence of those two great Christian leaders in a single baptistery later gave birth to a legend according to which, as Augustine emerged from the waters of baptism, he and Ambrose spontaneously composed the hymn that is now called the *Te Deum*.

Ostia

Augustine then decided to return to Africa, in order there to dedicate himself to a philosophical and contemplative life jointly with Adeodatus, Monica and a group of friends. But the usurper Maximus had blockaded the seaports, and Augustine had to remain for some time in Ostia, the place from which he expected to take ship to return to his native land. There Monica fell ill and died, but not before sharing with her son some of the joys of his new faith, in what has traditionally been called "the vision of Ostia."

> But because the day when she was to quit this life was drawing near—a day
> known to you, though we were ignorant of it—she and I happened to be
> alone, through the mysterious workings of your will, as I believe. We stood
> leaning against a window which looked out on a garden within the house
> where we were staying in Ostia on the Tiber, for there, far from the crowds,

we were recruiting our strength after the long journey, in preparation for our voyage overseas. We were alone, conferring very intimately. Forgetting what lay in the past, and stretching out to what was ahead, we inquired between ourselves in the light of present truth, the Truth which is yourself, what the eternal life of the saints would be like. Eye has not seen nor ear heard nor human heart conceived it, yet with the mouth of our hearts wide open we panted thirstily for the celestial streams of your fountain, the fount of life which is with you, that bedewed from it according to our present capacity we might in our little measure think upon a thing so great.

Our colloquy led us to the point where the pleasures of the body's senses, however intense and in however brilliant a material light enjoyed, seemed unworthy not merely of comparison but even of remembrance beside the joy of that life, and we lifted ourselves in longing yet more ardent toward *That Which Is*, and step by step traversed all bodily creatures and heaven itself, whence sun and moon and stars shed their light upon the earth. Higher still we mounted by inward thought and wondering discourse on your works, and we arrived at the summit of our own minds; and this too we transcended, to touch that land of never-failing plenty where you pasture Israel forever with the good of truth. . . . And as we talked and panted for it, we just touched the edge of it by the utmost leap of our hearts; then, sighing and unsatisfied, we left the first-fruits of our spirit captive there, and returned to the noise of articulate speech, where a word has beginning and end. How different from your Word, our Lord, who abides in himself, and grows not old, but renews all things.[27]

At the end of the conversation Monica told Augustine:

For my part, my son, I find pleasure no longer in anything this life holds. What I am doing here still, or why I tarry, I do not know, for all worldly hope has withered away for me. One thing only there was for which I desired to linger awhile in this life: to see you a Catholic Christian before I died. And this my God has granted to me more lavishly than I could have hoped, letting me see you even spurning earthly happiness to be his servant. What now keeps me here?[28]

A few days later, Monica died.

---

[27]*Confessions* 9.10.23-24. NCP I/1:226-28.
[28]*Confessions* 9.10.26. NCP I/1:229.

3

From the Baptistery
to the Pulpit

RETURN TO AFRICA

At the end of the ninth book of his *Confessions*, Augustine exalts Monica's virtues and expresses his feelings upon her death. Unfortunately, from there on the *Confessions* sets aside its former autobiographical character, so that the four books remaining tell us little about how his life and his thought developed. But it is also at that point in his life that Augustine began a vast literary production—including numerous letters—that allows us to follow the course of his life, as well as the development of his own thought and his understanding of Christian faith. Later on, his sermons would also provide interesting details about his life both before and after his ordination.

After burying Monica, Augustine and his companions returned to Rome, where they remained for several months until they were able to resume their trip to Africa, spend some time in Carthage and finally settle in the small town of Tagaste, where Augustine had spent his early years. He had now returned with a profound conviction that he was starting life anew. He had left Tagaste for Carthage, and then for Rome, with the hope of making a career for himself as a teacher of that rhetoric which was so admired by the Greco-Roman culture that his father represented. Now he returned, still immersed in the Neoplatonic atmosphere to which he had been led by his spiritual pilgrimage, but also baptized into his mother's faith. Monica had devoted her life to making of him a Christian, a member of the church and a partaker of its faith. Now Augustine returned to Tagaste as a baptized Christian, and this implied two things. It implied, first of all, that his life would no longer be that of a fully independent intellectual seeking truth with a group of friends. Now he was a member of the church. Upon receiving baptism, he had accepted and confessed the faith of that church. This meant that from that point on his thought should be grounded on that faith. Certainly, as years went by his thought would develop, change and be purified; but he would always seek to ground it on the gospel. Second, Augustine's return to Tagaste as a baptized Christian also meant that from then on he was called to lead others to faith, as his mother had done with him. He still carried with him the ideal—which he would never abandon—of living within an intimate community devoted to thought and devotion. But now this community had to include dimensions of service and teaching.

This new dimension may be seen in the letter he received from his friend Nebridius just a few months after returning to Tagaste.

> Is it true, my dear Augustine? Do you devote such energy and patience to the affairs of your fellow citizens, while you do not receive in turn that repose that you desire so much? Please, who are these people who make demands upon your goodness? I believe that they do not know what you love and what you long for. . . . I cry out, I testify that you love God and desire to serve him and cling to him. I would like to invite you to my country home and have you rest there. For I am not afraid of being labeled your seducer by your fellow citizens whom you love too much and by whom you are loved too much.[1]

Nebridius could not understand how Augustine could be concerned about "the affairs of your fellow citizens" when what he actually wished was to spend his time in meditation and philosophical dialogue. Shortly after having written this letter, he wrote several others to Augustine in which he posed profound philosophical questions. Augustine answered, because he had always been fascinated by such matters. But he did not

---

[1]*Letter* 5.1. NCP II/1:24.

do so as often nor as extensively as Nebridius would have wished. In one of his letters in the following year, Augustine tells Nebridius that he was unable to find the time or the leisure to think and discuss more fully the issues that before they found so fascinating.[2] And in the following year he would say that he did not have as much leisure as Nebridius thought, even though he still wished he did.[3]

OTHER EARLY WRITINGS

That shift in Augustine's interests and activities had already begun to take place from the time of his baptism and his mother's death, even before returning to Africa. While he awaited the opportunity to take ship to his native land, Augustine continued writing. Among the writings of those few months there is one, *On the Quantity of the Soul*, that shows much of the same methodology and concerns of his earlier writings, devoted to the philosophical quest for truth. But there are two others that seek to refute the errors of the Manichaeans—*On Free Will*, which he began then but did not complete until two years later, and *On the Catholic Way of Life*. In other words, the philosopher Augustine, the seeker of truth, is now also Augustine the theologian, the defender of truth against error. The same may be said of the works written in Tagaste, which include, among others, *On the Teacher* and *On Genesis Against the Manichaeans*.

Since later we shall have occasion to deal in more detail with Augustine's controversy with the Manichaeans and how this affected his own theology, it is not necessary to discuss here his treatise *On Genesis Against the Manichaeans*. But it is important to take a moment to consider *On the Teacher*, a writing whose influence was felt throughout the entire Middle Ages. As many others of Augustine's works at that time, this too is a dialogue. In this case his interlocutor is Adeodatus, who must have been about sixteen years old. Augustine later said that the words that this dialogue puts in the mouth of Adeodatus really came from him, and not from Augustine, which would seem to indicate that the young man's mind was quite comparable to his father's. A large section of the dialogue

---

[2]*Letter* 13.1.
[3]*Letter* 14.1.

consists in a discussion about the value of words, eventually to come to the conclusion that the words themselves teach nothing, for they are signs pointing to other realities; and if we do not know these realities, words themselves are meaningless: "The only way in which we have learned the words that we know, or may learn those that we do not know, is by perceiving their meaning, which does not come from the sound itself, but rather from the knowledge of that which they signify."[4] Therefore, "the manner in which we come to know the multitude of things in our mind is not by consulting the outer voice that speaks to us, but rather by consulting the inner truth that reigns in the spirit. . . . And that truth which is consulted and which teaches is Christ. . . . Every rational soul learns from this Wisdom."[5]

This is the fundamental vision behind Augustine's theory of knowledge as illumination. Following Plato and the Neoplatonists, Augustine is convinced that true knowledge is not that of visible and ephemeral realities, but that of the eternal and immutable. What we call "knowledge" is actually two things: First of all, the knowledge of mutable things, which is gathered by the senses and through observation, and which is properly called "science"—*scientia*. And second, there is the knowledge of immutable things, which goes beyond science, and is "wisdom"—*sapientia*. It is this knowledge, this wisdom, that truly interests Augustine. Such knowledge does not come through discovery or through the observation of things and how they work, which can never take us beyond things themselves. Where can it come from? For some time, Augustine flirted with the Platonic doctrine of the preexistence of souls, which would make it possible to explain present knowledge as a memory of the past. But once he had definitively abandoned the possibility of the preexistence of souls, he came to the conclusion that true knowledge comes to us through an illumination by Christ, the eternal Word of God. "The soul is like the eye, and God is like the light."[6] Just as the eye cannot see without light, the soul does not see without an illumination from on high.

---

[4] *On the Teacher* 11.36.
[5] *On the Teacher* 11.38.
[6] *On Sins and Their Remission* 1.25.

In all of this, Augustine was simply taking up the long Christian tradition (Justin, Clement, Origen) that saw the Word or Logos of God as the source of all knowledge, and expanding it to make it an entire theory of knowledge. That theory would become dominant in the following centuries and would rule the thought of Western Europe at least until the thirteenth century—to which we shall return.

But Augustine adds a practical or moral dimension to this theory of knowledge. In order to attain such illumination, the soul must be purified. The philosophers of his time frequently declared that the goal of knowledge is virtue: that one can only live according to truth when one understands it. The same was said by the Manichaeans, who held that their doctrines were the only rational explanation of the nature of the world, and that therefore they were the only foundation for a wise and virtuous life. In contrast, Augustine saw virtue as a necessary element in order to attain truth. In his book *On the Usefulness of Believing*, which he wrote after his ordination as a presbyter as an attempt to refute several Manichaean tenets, Augustine declares this quite radically: "To wish to see the truth in the hope of purifying the spirit is to invert the order of things, putting first what should be last; it is necessary to purify in order to see."[7] In another writing, also addressing the Manichaeans, he affirms that in order to reach knowledge both diligence and piety are required.[8] Diligence leads one to seek those who can truly teach. But even when the most excellent teachers are found one cannot learn what they teach without first practicing piety and virtue.

Thus true knowledge requires two things, just as sight requires two. In order to see properly, the eye must be clear and healthy. A sick eye cannot see well. Likewise, in order to know truth—in order to reach wisdom—the soul has to practice virtue; it has to be healed from every disease that impedes it from seeing the truth. But the eye cannot see if there is not also an external illumination. Without that illumination, things are distorted—as with the child who sees monsters in the darkness of night. Likewise, the virtuous soul cannot see by itself, but needs an illumination.

---

[7]*On the Usefulness of Believing* 16.34.
[8]*On the Customs of the Catholic Church* 1.1.

This is the light of God, whose function in the knowledge of eternal truth is similar to the function of sunlight in the knowledge of the temporal.

Thus, while agreeing with Plato that the senses cannot lead to true knowledge, Augustine proposes a theory that avoids the Platonic doctrine of the preexistence of souls.

> That noble philosopher Plato tried to persuade us that the souls of men had lived even before they wore these bodies, and therefore learning things is more a remembering of things already known than a getting to know new things. . . . The conclusion we should rather draw is that the nature of the intellectual mind has been so established by the disposition of its creator that it is subjoined to intelligible things in the order of nature, and so it sees such truths in a kind of non-bodily light that is *sui generis*, just as our eyes of flesh see all these things that lie around us in this bodily light, a light they were created to be receptive of and to match.[9]

MONASTIC LIFE

While Augustine was writing these works he was also enjoying and organizing the community that he had formed in Tagaste with his friends and Adeodatus. In contrast to what had been the nature of the Cassiciacum community—and of what Nebridius thought was to be an ideal community—this new community would not limit itself to devotion and spiritual conversation, but would also serve the rest of the faithful and strengthen them in the faith by refuting the many errors that circulated in the area. It would also have its rules whose purpose would be to encourage love and its expression, as well as to discipline the life of the community. All this was to be done under the leadership of Augustine himself. Thus one may well say that Augustine founded a sort of monastery that worked under his direction. He had always admired those great athletes of the faith, the monks of the Egyptian desert—particularly St. Anthony—for their discipline and readiness to abandon the pomp of the world. About those monks he would write enthusiastic words, idealizing life in the desert.

---

[9] *On the Trinity* 12.24. NCP I/5:335-36.

But if this sort of life goes beyond what we can tolerate, who would not admire and praise those men who, having held in contempt and abandoned the allurements of this world, have joined together in a common life that is most holy and most chaste, and who pass their life together in prayer, in reading, in discussion, not swollen with pride, not restless out of stubbornness, not livid with envy? Rather, they live modestly, reverently, and peacefully offer a life that is most harmonious and entirely directed toward God as a most pleasing sacrifice to him from whom they have merited the ability to live in that way. No one owns anything as his own; no one is burdensome to anyone. They produce by their hands what can nourish the body but cannot hold the mind back from God.[10]

But in contrast to those monks of the desert, among whom even the possession of a book was forbidden, and who withdrew from the rest of society, the life of the Tagaste community should include study as well as teaching and service to those around them. It would seem that Augustine's models for this were some of the urban monastic communities that he had seen in Milan and Rome.

I saw at Milan a house of holy men, not few in number, over whom one priest, an excellent and most learned man, presided. I know that there are also many houses in Rome in which individuals who excel in gravity, prudence, and the knowledge of God preside over the others who dwell with them and live in Christian love, holiness and freedom.[11]

Quite likely two of the communities in Rome of which Augustine had also heard were the feminine communities founded by two well-to-do women, Paula and Marcella, who in 282 asked Jerome, who had just arrived in Rome, to instruct them on the Bible and its languages. In the communities founded by these two women monasticism took a new twist, now centering, not so much on the mortification of the flesh, but rather on study and on a firm but reasonable austerity. This was the sort of community that Augustine founded in Tagaste.

---

[10]*On the Catholic Way of Life* 1.31.67. NCP I/19:61.
[11]*On the Catholic Way of Life* 1.33.70. NCP I/19:63.

Even though moving far beyond our narrative, this may be the best moment to say something about Augustine's contribution to monastic life. When he was forced to accept being a priest in Hippo, Augustine agreed as long as he was allowed to continue the community lifestyle he had established in Tagaste. Employing a property that Bishop Valerius assigned to that task, Augustine then began there a new community of study and devotion, composed mostly of members of the clergy. Later, when Augustine became bishop of Hippo, he preferred that all his clergy should be members of that community.

One often reads about the "Rule of St. Augustine" as if Augustine himself had written legislation for monastic communities. The truth is that in the Latin West there was no successful monastic rule until St. Benedict wrote his, approximately in 529. What is then called the "Rule of St. Augustine" is in fact a later compilation of elements of monastic life that are indeed to be found in the writings of Augustine, but that he never combined into a rule. The main documents allowing us to see how Augustine understood and organized monastic life are his epistle 211 and his sermons 355 and 356. The first of these is a letter that Augustine wrote to a feminine monastic community under the leadership of his sister, whose name is unknown, but whom tradition has dubbed Perpetua. Apparently there had been some dissension among those nuns, and Augustine wrote calling them to greater unity. He bemoans the fact that while the church boasts of its unity over against the Donatists there are inner schisms in a monastic community. The letter is followed by a series of principles that are the heart of what later became the Rule of Augustine. The two sermons just mentioned are responses to criticisms against the community that Augustine led in Hippo, and therefore allow a glimpse of that community. Let us look first at the essential points of the Rule.

One of the pillars of a monastic community is to be common property. No one is to claim anything as private property, but everything is to be at the disposal of all. This is absolutely necessary for the good order of the community, for without it there would be debates and envy over what one owns. But Augustine agrees with the general tenor of most of the great monastic founders in the Latin West, that monks and nuns are not to live in extreme poverty, nor mortify the flesh to an excess. On the contrary, it is important that all have the necessary food and clothing. This will require a common place for food and clothing from which each will take whatever is needed. Both clothing and food are to be simple, with set times for fasting and for abstinence from meat or wine. But if someone is ill that person is to receive special food and care. There will also be a common library, once again at the disposal of all. There will be set periods for community prayer, at which all must be present, but when such common prayer is not taking place the oratory must be kept free so that any who wish to go there for private prayer may do so. Furthermore, all are to work, although Augustine does not determine how.

The matter of property was not a simple one for Augustine and the monastic community in Hippo. This may be seen clearly in the two sermons mentioned above. They show that there were several problems and criticisms. For example, the priest Januarius had retained some property in the name of his son and his daughter, who had both joined the monastic communities. Augustine did not know of this until he was told by some who disliked the community itself. Even then the matter was complicated, for there were profound disagreements between the two children of Januarius. Deacon Severus had bought a house for his mother and his sister, and he had done this by combining a personal loan with some money received as offerings from believers. Who then owned that property? Once again there were serious disagreements between Severus and his mother. These cases, like many others of the same sort, required the intervention of Augustine, who had to solve them in such a way that people such as Severus's mother would not be left in poverty, but at the same time the principle of the community of goods would be preserved. Obviously clergy who were married presented even greater difficulties.

As a consequence of such difficulties, Augustine decided that those among his clergy who wished to abandon the common life of the monastery could do so, although he himself would not be too happy about it, considering it not a sin but certainly a failure. But while he was not happy with those who would decide to retain their personal property and to abandon the community, he would not depose them from their pastoral functions, but rather let God be their judge.

For these reasons, Augustine wished for the church to have as little property as possible. When a rich merchant by the name of Boniface intended to make the church the heir of his shipping company, so that the church would always have resources and a certain measure of security, Augustine rejected the legacy, which while providing a measure of security for the church would also have forced it to go into the shipping business.

> It is not right for us to keep a reserve fund; it's not the bishop's business to save up gold, and repulse the beggar's outstretched hand. There are so many asking every day, so many groaning, so many needy people pleading, that we have to leave several of them unhappy, because we haven't got enough to give all of them something; and should we set up a fund to insure against shipwreck?[12]

The second pillar of monastic life must be obedience. In his letter to the nuns, Augustine exhorts them to obey their superior as the mother who conceived them, not in her womb, but in her spirit. But while insisting on obedience, Augustine seems to take for granted that the basis for the authority of a prior or prioress is not their having been assigned to that position but their holiness, their wisdom and their charisma. As we shall see further on, this was the manner in which traditional North African culture understood authority, in contrast to the Roman attitude, which understood that authority resided not so much in an individual's character as in the function to which that person had been assigned. Later, Western monasticism, following the Roman tradition, took care in determining how people in authority were to be elected and what was to be their authority.

Since this seemed the best place to discuss Augustine's contribution to monastic life, in this section, while beginning with the community that he founded in Tagaste, and then the one in Hippo, we have moved

---

[12]*Sermon* 355.5. NCP III/10:168.

far beyond the chronology of his life. Thus it is best now to return to the narrative of Augustine's life.

Hippo

Returning to our story, the years in Tagaste were not free from grief and difficulties, particularly the deaths of Adeodatus and Nebridius. But Augustine remained firm in his conviction that it was to this life that God had called him, and in which he expected to spend the remainder of his days. His writings and teachings were spreading far and wide, and people often came to him to help discern truth and justice when issues were being disputed. Since he was afraid of being forced to become a pastor, he avoided visiting places where the bishopric was vacant.

Then he received an entreaty from the city of Hippo, north of Tagaste on the Mediterranean shores. A public functionary was asking him how to organize in his city a community similar to the one in Tagaste, and Augustine decided to go there. While he was in Hippo he attended public worship led by Bishop Valerius. Valerius was a wise elderly man who, as we are told by Posidius in his *Life of Saint Augustine*, "spoke to the faithful about the need to find and ordain a presbyter for the city." As was to be expected, and as Valerius fully intended, the faithful,

> who already knew the way of life and the teachings of St. Augustine, who was among the audience without imagining what might happen, . . . seized him, and as is usually done in such cases, presented him to Valerius to be ordained, requesting this with great clamor and earnest desires. All of them, except Augustine, who wept abundantly.[13]

According to his biographer, some took his weeping to be due to frustration because he had hoped to be a bishop and now would be made a presbyter; but Augustine himself later told him that he wept because he was "thinking of the many and grave perils to which his life would now be exposed, devoted to the leadership and rule of the church."[14]

---

[13] Posidius, *Life of Saint Augustine* 4.
[14] Ibid.

Augustine's refusal to be ordained, and then being forced into acceptance, was not a situation unheard of. His own mentor, Ambrose, when the people acclaimed him as their bishop, fled and hid, and it was necessary for the emperor to issue an order so that he would accept the office to which he was being called. Some thirty years before Augustine, Gregory of Nazianzus had a similar experience, and finally yielded, accepted ordination and displayed his sentiments in a famous homily that began with the words: "I have been conquered, and I confess my defeat." As to Augustine, in a letter to Valerius written after his ordination, he said:

> The second post at the helm was handed to me who did not yet know how to hold an oar.
>
> But I think that my Lord wanted to correct me in that way precisely because I dared, as if I were more learned and better, to reprimand the mistakes of many sailors before I had experienced what is involved in their work. And so, after I was launched into the middle of the sea, I began to feel the rashness of my reprimands, though even earlier I judged this ministry to be filled with perils. And this was the reason for those tears that some of the brothers noticed that I shed in the city at the time of my ordination.[15]

Apparently Valerius was taking other matters into consideration. The two great challenges before him as bishop of Hippo were Manichaeism and Donatism. Who could better refute Manichaeism than this famous ex-Manichaean, now converted to Christian faith? As to Donatism, its great strength was among the Punic and Berber population, particularly in the rural areas but also in the very city of Hippo. The presence and strength of Donatism in Hippo was such that when the Donatist bishop ordered bakers not to serve orthodox Christians, his command created grave difficulties for the latter. Valerius himself was more comfortable in Greek and could hardly preach in Latin. As a mestizo, Augustine had an excellent formation in Latin rhetoric and, although he did not speak the native tongue easily, at least he knew it, and through his mother he belonged to that ancient African culture in which Donatism was making headway. Furthermore, Valerius was proud of the presbyter he had captured. He soon

---

[15]*Letter* 21.1-2. NCP II/1:55.

put Augustine in charge of teaching the people and—something that was usually not done—allowed him to preach in the presence of Valerius himself. (Some years before, Origen had been forced to abandon his native city of Alexandria because he had dared preach before bishops.) Although other bishops criticized him for this, Valerius remained firm, so that two years later Augustine, who was still a presbyter, preached before all the bishops of the province who were gathered in Hippo under the leadership of Aurelius, bishop of Carthage. Later, Aurelius would become Augustine's main ally in the struggle against Donatism. But Valerius was not content with this, and went to Aurelius asking that Augustine be made a coadjutor bishop. This was forbidden by the canons of the Council of Nicaea, which decreed that there should never be more than one bishop in a single city. But thanks to Valerius's insistence, in 395 Augustine was consecrated as coadjutor bishop of Valerius, who died in the following year, leaving Augustine as the bishop of the city.

PASTORAL TASKS

First as a presbyter, but particularly after he became a bishop, Augustine had many and different tasks. He was to preside over the preparation of candidates for baptism—the catechumens. Although part of that instruction was in the hands of others, as the date of baptism approached (normally Easter or Pentecost), Bishop Augustine had to take charge of the last steps in the catechumenate. The last weeks of preparation for baptism were devoted to what was called the *traditio et reditio symboli*—the giving and returning of the creed. This was the creed of Nicaea, established in 325 by the Council of Nicaea, and generally accepted as a common sign of orthodoxy. During these last weeks before Easter, as they prepared for baptism, what the bishop was to teach the catechumens was this creed and its meaning, for at their baptism they would be asked to affirm it, and therefore it was important that they understood its meaning and significance, and that they were able to explain it at least in simple terms. Furthermore, it was the bishop's task to make sure that each candidate for baptism lived and behaved according to the faith that he or she would embrace in baptism.

Likewise, Bishop Augustine had to preach and preside over Communion, which was the center of Christian worship. As long as he was a presbyter it would be usual for Augustine to serve as an aide to Valerius in the main church in the city, or as his representative in other churches. But, as we have seen, Augustine's fame was such that while he was still a presbyter Valerius had him preach in his presence, and soon other bishops did likewise. After becoming a bishop, he would preside over worship in that central church and be responsible for preaching in it. Many of his sermons still exist, usually as the result of notes taken by his audience. In them we see Augustine as a shepherd seeking to feed his flock and to instruct and correct it when necessary. When we read them today, particularly in some of the more traditional and stilted translations, it is difficult to see both their literary beauty and their spontaneity, and therefore to understand the impact of Augustine's sermons on his audience. In one of his letters, Augustine tells his friend Alypius of his concern that on feast days devoted to the memory and honor of martyrs people would go to their tombs and there celebrate with gluttony, drinking and debauchery. These practices combined Christian elements with others of pagan origins, for pagan religious festivities were frequently celebrated with banquets and drunkenness, and Christians—at least since the second century—had long followed the custom of celebrating Communion at the tombs of martyrs as a way of showing that they were part of a single church. Now many combined the two, celebrating the feasts of the martyrs as they used to celebrate pagan feasts. As was to be expected, Augustine did not approve of the gluttony and drunkenness at the martyrs' tombs, and preached several sermons against such practices. At first, there was much opposition to what he said. But eventually he won over most of his congregation, which broke into tears. At this point, Augustine tells Alypius, "I did not evoke their tears with my tears, but when I said such things, I admit, I was caught up in their weeping and could not hold back my own. And when we had both equally wept, I brought my sermon to an end with the fullest hope of their correction."[16] Thus those sermons that to us may seem cold and

---

[16]*Letter* 29.7. NCP II/1:98.

excessively long had a profound emotional dimension that shook the
hearts of those who heard them.

his pastoral task was visiting the sick, consoling the
e disheartened, chastising the proud and accompany-
cial times in their lives such as marriage and death.
e the practice of private confession had not become
no doubt that as a pastor Augustine had to chastise,
se who in some manner fell into sin or strayed away
life required.

Then there were administrative tasks, which included the supervision of other ministers and functionaries of the church as well as the
management of the economic resources and properties of the church.
As to the first, the bishop had to supervise the presbyters who represented him in other churches in the city and its surroundings. It was
understood that in the city there should be only one church, presided
over and led by a bishop. But since not all could attend services in the
central church or cathedral where the bishop preached and celebrated
Communion, it was necessary to have other meeting places. There a
presbyter would preside over worship and preach, but he would do this
in the name of the bishop. Therefore one of the main responsibilities
of the bishop was to make certain that each presbyter was his worthy
representative both in behavior and in teaching. The semimonastic
community that Augustine had founded in Hippo, and to which he
belonged throughout his life, came to occupy an important place in
this context, for it was there that his teachings were discussed and
preaching was formulated and discussed. It is well to remember that
although the previous community in Tagaste was devoted to study and
devotion, there was already there an emphasis on the need to serve
others. In transporting these practices to Hippo, and relating them to
his own pastoral tasks, Augustine turned that community into a center
where those who were to serve the church as elders and other officers
were formed.

Since there were other functionaries or ministers in the church, their
supervision also was the responsibility of the bishop. First, besides the

bishop and the presbyters, there were the deacons, who would help the bishop and the elders in the leadership of worship, and who apparently were the ones offering the chalice to the faithful in the Communion service. Their main responsibility was to be in charge of the philanthropic work of the church and therefore to a great measure to be in charge of just about all the economic resources of the church—a subject to which we shall return shortly. The "hostiary" was so called because among his other responsibilities he took care of the hosts for Communion. But the hostiary was actually a guardian or doorman who was in charge of the cleanliness of the church building and of order in the worship service. He was also responsible for making sure that only those who were supposed to partake of Communion did so. The "readers" were mostly young men aspiring to become presbyters, and who were preparing for that position by reading Scripture out loud in the worship service—although there are some indications that the reading of the Gospels was reserved for the deacons. "Exorcists" too were frequently candidates to the presbyterate, although older than the readers. Their responsibilities included praying for the catechumens preparing for baptism, expelling the demons of their past life. They were also responsible for ministry among the "energoumens," that is, people supposedly possessed by demons and for whose healing the exorcists prayed. The "subdeacons," besides helping in the celebration of worship—in which they were also called "acolytes"—were helpers or secretaries to the bishop, who frequently had to send several copies of the same letter or document to several people. All of these people the bishop was to supervise and teach, for his main responsibility was to make certain that all performed their functions—particularly preaching, teaching and the administration of goods and resources—on the basis of a clear understanding of the gospel. Ambrose, Augustine's mentor, had written the treatise *On the Duties of the Clergy*, where he began by affirming that his main task was to teach, but that in order to teach he had to learn: "As I seek to teach, I must also learn. For it was only the true Teacher who did not have to learn what he taught us. But all humans have to learn before they teach, and to receive from him what we are to bequeath to others."[17] The consequence of all this was that, although Augustine had wanted to devote all his time to study since the days of Cassiciacum, now as a pastor and a bishop his studies had an added dimension. It was not only now a matter of studying for the love of truth, or as an act of devotion, but also of studying as preparation to teach others.

Even so, a bishop's responsibilities were not limited to all that has been mentioned above. By that time the church had begun to hold properties given or bequeathed as inheritance by some of the faithful. Such properties required management. This was a task that Augustine did not cherish and that he delegated to some among his most trustworthy helpers. As his biographer says, only once a year would he ask for an account of what had been done with the properties and the income of the church. That income was employed both to support Augustine and his helpers and to provide aid to the poor. Although other bishops would do it, Augustine refused to employ the income from the properties of the church in order to buy other properties, insisting that all that was available should be employed in support of the needy. Furthermore, being acutely aware of the rumors and criticisms that the management of such possessions provoked, more than once he proposed to the membership at large that the clergy should get rid of such income and that the people themselves should commit to supporting the work of the church. But the faithful repeatedly rejected such an idea.

In these administrative tasks, Augustine called for clergy as well as for all believers to make good use of their possessions, while declaring that possessions that are not well used are not true possessions, for they are unjust.

> Everything, then, that is wrongly possessed is someone else's property, but one who uses it wrongly possesses it wrongly. You see, then, how many people ought to return the property of others, if at least a few people are found to whom they might return it. These people, wherever they are, hold these things more in contempt to the extent that they could possess them with more justice. No one, of course, wrongly possesses justice, and

---

[17] Ambrose, *On the Duties of the Clergy* 1.1.3.

one who does not love it does not have it. But money is both wrongly possessed by bad people and possessed by good people in a better way to the extent that it is loved less.[18]

According to Augustine, the rightful employment of goods, which is the foundation of their rightful possession, must be grounded on the distinction between enjoying and using.

> So then, there are some things which are meant to be enjoyed, others which are meant to be used, yet others which do both the enjoying and the using. Things that are to be enjoyed make us happy; things which are to be used help us on our way to happiness, providing us, so to say, with crutches and props for reaching the things that will make us happy, and enabling us to keep them.
>
> We ourselves, however, both enjoy and use things, and find ourselves in the middle, in a position to choose which to do. So if we wish to enjoy things that are meant to be used, we are impeding our own progress, and sometimes are also deflected from our course, because we are thereby delayed in obtaining what we should be enjoying, or turned back from it altogether, blocked by our love for inferior things.[19]

Since only God produces true enjoyment, the use of all things is to be directed to that end: enjoying God. When this does not take place, use becomes abuse, and therefore possession becomes unjust and illicit—even though the civil law may justify it.

It was on this principle that Augustine sought to build his entire administrative policy. If it is wrong for individuals to make wrong use of their goods, using them to seek enjoyment of other goods rather than the enjoyment of God, it is much worse for the church to do likewise. The manner in which all things are to be used is, after meeting all absolute necessities, to employ them for the good of the needy. Those who insist on enjoying what is only to be used, as if its purpose were to enjoy other things, fall into idolatry, for they seek in things a joy that can only be attained in God.

---

[18]*Letter* 153.26. NCP II/2:404.
[19]*On Christian Doctrine* 1.3. NCP I/11.103.

This is why Augustine insisted that the leaders of the church should not use more than what was necessary, and that all that was left over should then be employed to help the needy, which leads to the enjoyment of God. And it was for the same reason that he repeatedly proposed that the church should rid itself of all its properties, giving them to the poor, and that pastors should not receive the income from such properties, but only the offerings of the faithful—and even these offerings were to be used for the clergy only to the point of meeting the immediate needs of food, clothing and shelter, for anything beyond that should also be employed in works of charity.

As to legacies left to the church, Augustine would reject them if they did not seem just—as in the case of a father who would leave his property to the church as a vengeful act against his children, whom he thus disinherited—and would accept them only as a way to have more resources to help the needy. He always insisted that the majority of the income of the church should be employed to support the poor and widows, and that the clergy should live in such a manner that they could not be accused of living at the expense of the people. This was to be seen in the manner in which they dressed themselves, which should not be ostentatious in its luxury nor in its excessive show of poverty. (At worship, clergy were to dress in the same manner as the rest of the people, although there were some who had an extra change of clothing that they reserved for presiding at Communion.) A similar attitude was to prevail at meals, which would include legumes, wine and sometimes meat, but with no luxury, and where a sober behavior was expected. It is said that when some sitting at the table with him did not show sufficient decorum they were fined by being deprived of their allotment of wine. (And it is also said that he kept at the table a sign saying: "Any who with their words would chew on the life of others are not worthy to sit at this table.")

There were still other important tasks. One that would increasingly occupy his time was lending support and guidance to his colleagues in other parts of the empire. Sometimes he would travel to another city in order to sit at a council, although normally he would write long letters dealing with the doubts and questions of his colleagues, or he would take the initiative in admonishing someone whose life or doctrine did not seem appropriate. It was this task of responding to questions and doubts that produced the enormous correspondence of which only part is still extant, which even so fills several volumes. Many of his most important theological treatises were written in response to a colleague requesting arguments against a particular error—mostly those of the Manichaeans, Donatists and Pelagians, whom we shall treat in future chapters.

Still another sort of task had to do with civil matters. Although these issues were supposed to be the responsibility of civil authorities, they often ended up on the bishop's shoulders. Posidius says that Augustine would "communicate in correspondence with some who consulted with him on temporal matters. But he took this heavy burden as a distraction."[20]

These temporal occupations were not limited to questions posed by distant correspondents. The administration of justice by civil authorities had reached such a state of corruption that many did not trust it, and would go to respected leaders of the church to ask them to settle their differences and disagreements. Many years before he became a bishop, while he was still living in Milan, Augustine had the experience of wishing to speak with Bishop Ambrose about his own doubts and anxieties, and not being able to do it because Ambrose was so thoroughly occupied by the many issues that came before him. Soon Augustine found himself in similar circumstances, for he had to give audience to many who came to see him, not for religious matters, but to ask for his judgment over a matter under debate. Also about this Posidius—who was part of the monastic community until he was elected bishop of Calama in 397—says that "sometimes the audiences lasted until dinner time; and sometimes he would fast through the entire day, listening to issues and solving them."[21] In his sermons there are abundant echoes of these activities, including the many suits he had to hear and adjudicate—for instance, among relatives disputing over an inheritance. One may well imagine that a good portion of those who came to the bishop for

---

[20]Posidius, *Life of Saint Augustine* 19.
[21]Posidius, *Life of Saint Augustine* 20.

judgment were people of African race and traditions who did not trust the Roman authorities, and who saw Augustine as closer to them.

In brief, the life of a conscientious bishop such as Augustine was neither easy nor lived in abundance. This makes his vast theological and literary output even more surprising and admirable.

4

The Shepherd and
the Manichaeans

For nine years Augustine was a Manichaean. When he finally accepted Monica's faith and received baptism from the hands of Ambrose, he felt the need to refute the teachings that he had formerly followed and defended. Thus many of his writings—particularly the earlier ones—sought to refute Manichaeism. And, as is often the case, that task of rebuttal also left an imprint on the theology of Augustine himself, who developed many of his ideas in opposition to Manichaeism. Therefore, in order to understand Augustine's thought it is necessary to understand something of Manichaeism, of its attraction and of Augustine's refutation.

MANICHAEISM

Manichaeism originated in Persia. Its name is derived from its founder, Mani. Mani came to the conviction that the main religions that he knew in Persia—Zoroastrianism, Buddhism and Christianity—represented a divine process of revelation whose high point was Mani himself. Intrigued by Buddhism, he went to live in India for some time, and upon returning to Persia he sought to convince the leaders of that land to follow the religion that he now proposed as the culmination of the three great ancient religions. But he did not succeed in this, and fleeing persecution from Zoroastrian authorities in Persia he sought refuge in India. After some time he returned to Persia, still insisting on the superiority of the religion whose representative he was. Having been condemned as a subversive by Persian authorities, who supported the religion of Zoroaster, Mani was beheaded and skinned. His skin, filled with straw, was then exposed publicly as a warning to any who might consider following him.

Mani died in 273, some hundred years before Augustine would embrace some of his teachings. Meanwhile his disciples, fleeing persecution in Persia, had scattered through the neighboring region and much farther—to the point that Manichaean documents have been found as far as China. As part of that expansion, Manichaeism entered the Roman Empire. In these lands, its main success was in Alexandria, where there had been a long tradition of various sorts of syncretism quite similar to what Mani proposed. This tradition had always held—following Plato— that true religion can only be reached by a limited number of people who are particularly rational. Therefore, Manichaeism, which claimed to be such a profoundly rational system that only superior minds could understand it, found a fertile field in Alexandria. From there it passed on to Italy and to what were then the provinces of Africa and Numidia— today Tunisia and part of Algeria—where during Augustine's lifetime it was one of the main rivals of Christianity.

Using words and notions that were Christian in origin, Mani had claimed that he was the Paraclete or "other comforter" that Jesus had promised, and therefore his disciples saw in his teachings the supreme revelation of God. But at the same time that Manichaeism claimed to be the product of divine revelation, it was a sort of rationalism that claimed to be able to explain all the mysteries of the universe. This was its main attraction among educated people in the Greco-Roman world, many of whom were disillusioned with the traditional religion of the land precisely because it was not sufficiently rational. This was the reason why Augustine became interested in Manichaeism. And it was also the failure of such claims that eventually led Augustine to abandon it.

Although in its beginnings and in its most traditional form Manichaeism was a highly intellectual system whose allure was in its claim that everything could be explained by rational means, without accepting the authority of what others had said, there soon appeared another sort of Manichaean who believed that the entire system should be accepted, not just because of the force of its reasoning, but because of the authority of the great prophet Mani. Augustine and his study companions in Carthage, as well as later his Manichaean friends in Milan, were of the traditional sort, for whom the attractiveness of Manichaeism was in the rational response it seemed to give to the most difficult questions having to do both with human existence and with the order of the universe.

In the Roman province of Africa, in places such as Tagaste and Hippo, Augustine soon had to face more extreme Manichaeans, for whom the teachings of Mani were infallible, and who had scarcely given any thought to what they claimed to believe but were perfectly convinced that their interpretation of Christianity as well as of all of reality was the true and only possible one. Therefore, although the true followers of Manichaeism were always few, and were regarded askance by authorities, some of their doctrines attracted many among the Christian population who were told that Manichaeism offered the correct interpretation of the person and teachings of Jesus, and that the church and its believers did not know the deeper dimensions of those teachings.

The great question that the Manichaeans claimed to have solved was the nature and origin of evil. As we have seen, Augustine could neither understand nor accept that a single good God could have made this world in which there is so much evil. The struggle within his own soul made it clear to him that evil existed even within himself. Mani and his followers solved this difficulty by declaring that there is not a single god creator of all things, but rather two equal principles, both eternal and indestructible, the principle of light and the principle of darkness. In the present world these two principles are intermingled and often even confused. Here, matter is the result of darkness, while all that is spiritual is like many bits of light captured within the darkness of the material. The human problem—as well as the cosmic drama—is then the very presence of darkness in the spiritual world, or the imprisonment of light in the material world. The clearest case of this is the human being, in whom a spiritual soul that is light is trapped within a material body that is darkness and that is therefore ruled by the principle of evil. Since in the classical understanding the very idea of "soul" is that which moves every living being, there is in a human being—just as in all living beings—a "soul" that gives life to the body. But this is a material soul. There is a higher soul, a spiritual one, which is held prisoner in a body, which is given life by the soul of darkness.

This mixture of light and darkness exists throughout the cosmos, and therefore Manichaeans sought to explain the movements of the heavenly bodies and all that took place within them on the basis of this principle of the admixture of light and darkness. Thus, for instance, they would explain the phases of the moon by saying that the moon was lightened by souls on their way returning to the realm of pure light. It was statements such as this that made it possible for this religion to appear scientifically rational. It was also one of the elements that made it most vulnerable to rational criticism, for the better astronomers had more exact explanations for such phenomena as the phases of the moon and the various celestial movements.

Furthermore, since the principle of darkness is just as eternal as the principle of light, the final victory of good will not be a destruction of darkness, but simply its expulsion from the realm of light. In other words, the future that the Manichaeans promised was a total separation between the spiritual reality of light and the material reality of darkness.

As to human beings, their salvation consists in freeing that spark of light that is in them from the prison of bodily matter. This is achieved through a strict ethics based on the principle of the "three seals": that is, the seal of the mouth, the seal of the hand and the seal of the heart. The seal of the mouth is on the one hand a series of dietetic principles enforcing a strict vegetarianism and abstinence from wine. And on the other hand the seal of the mouth means that nothing will come out of it such as blasphemy, untruth or curses—which reminds us of the saying of Jesus that what contaminates a human being is not what enters through the mouth, but what comes from it. The seal of the hand forbids violence against others as well as stealing and doing manual labor—which gives us a hint as to the aristocratic tendencies of Manichaeism. It also forbids having more than is necessary, which is limited to nourishment—again, all of vegetable origin—and a change of clothing a year. Finally, the seal of the heart—or of the chest—forbids contributing to the imprisonment of light within darkness. At a personal level, this means that the believer must make every effort to free the soul from the prison of the body, and this to such an extreme that the supreme action of Manichaean devotion was the *endura*, a rite in which the "perfect" gain eternal life by fasting to the point of death. But it also meant that procreation is sin, for it means that a new spark of light will be imprisoned in darkness. Therefore Manichaeans, while preferring celibacy and virginity, would insist any sexual act must be performed in such a way that there will be no progeny. (It is interesting to note that Adeodatus, Augustine's only son, was born before his father became a Manichaean, which would seem to indicate that after his conversion to Manichaeism Augustine began practicing some of the contraceptive methods that were then employed.)

All of this does not mean that it is possible for a spiritual soul to be eternally lost. The very nature of the soul is light, and darkness cannot prevail over light. What does happen is that some souls—at present, most of them—allow themselves to be obfuscated by the body and by matter, and forget their true nature. Such souls are condemned to return to the cycle of a life subjected to matter until they attain their liberation from the reign of darkness.

All this implies that in the final instance, whoever does evil does not do so out of a personal decision but out of a spiritual soul that is obfuscated by darkness and materiality. This material reality, and not knowing one's own nature, is what moves people to do evil. Those who do evil have no other remedy than to await the moment when they can understand their own spiritual nature to such a point that they will be able to obey the principle of light that resides in it. It is then through the knowledge of truth that one reaches this liberation that is salvation. After abandoning Manichaeism, Augustine would underscore the contrast between this and Christian doctrine, saying that "to wish . . . to see truth in order to purify the spirit is to invert the order and to postpone that which should appear first: purification is necessary in order to be able to see."[1]

---

[1] *On the Usefulness of Believing* 16.34.

As to its organization, Manichaeism had a hierarchical structure that included its leaders as well as the rest of believers. At the top of this hierarchy were the twelve "children of sweetness," under whom there was a tripartite hierarchy that was similar to the Christian system of bishops, presbyters and deacons. Among believers there were the "elect" and the "hearers." Upon the death of the body, the elect would return to the reign of light, while the hearers would be reincarnate in another person until they reached the level of the elect.

Also as part of this doctrine, Mani included Christ as the last great revelation of God before Mani himself. According to Mani, Christ was a purely celestial being, pure light in which the material body was a mere appearance that would allow him to communicate with those who are still prisoners of their own matter. Therefore Mani's Christology followed the same docetic scheme as that of the earlier Gnostics.

The attractiveness of Manichaeism was, first of all, in its claim to be able to explain in a rational way all the mysteries of the universe, and to do this on the basis of a revelation that itself provided the clue for that interpretation. Second, Manichaeism attracted intellectuals—particularly those from the higher echelons of society—because it led them to believe that their own knowledge and their own religiosity were a sign of their superiority over the rest. To be a Manichaean would imply that a person's soul had reached a higher level than those other souls that were not ready to reach the same intellectual heights.

What led Augustine to Manichaeism was that Monica's faith seemed irrational and even superstitious, while Manichaeism explained matters in a more rational way. And what led him to abandon it was his disappointment upon seeing that the supposedly wise men among the Manichaeans were mere charlatans who spoke well and said little. Some time later Augustine would say about the intellectual claims of the Manichaeans that "they accuse the Catholic Church because it requires that those who come to it believe, while they claim that they do not impose on any the yoke of faith, but rather open to them the fountainhead of science."[2] This is why it was important for Augustine to show the vacuity

---

[2]*On the Usefulness of Believing* 9.21.

of that famous Manichaean teacher Faustus, who supposedly would dispel all his doubts, and how this began leading him away from Manichaeism: "I heard the man for whom we awaited as if he were to be sent from heaven so that he would clarify those matters which had us quite confused, and saw he was like the rest, with the exception of a certain degree of eloquence."[3]

AUGUSTINE'S WRITINGS AGAINST THE MANICHAEANS

Augustine wrote extensively against the Manichaeans. Almost immediately after becoming a Christian, he wrote two works with that purpose in mind: *The Catholic Way of Life and the Manichean Way of Life* and *On Genesis, Against the Manicheans*. The first sought to respond to the claims of the Manichaeans about their own austerity and holiness. While Augustine argued that Manichaean austerity was not all that it seemed to be, he also confessed that there were also bad Christians, but this does not mean that Christianity is false. Shortly after being trapped by Valerius into becoming a presbyter, Augustine held in Hippo a debate with a noted Manichaean teacher by the name of Fortunatus. The record of this debate is still extant. About this debate, Augustine's biographer Posidius says that Christians, orthodox or Catholic as well as Donatists, asked Augustine to refute Fortunatus, and that he accepted. Posidius tells us:

> Once the day and place were set, the gathering took place with a great attendance of studious people as well as the curious. The tables were prepared for notaries, and the discussion began, continuing until the second day. As one may see in the acts of this conference, the Manichean teacher was unable to refute the claims of Christian doctrine and also to build that of Mani on some solid bases. At the end, without knowing what to do, he sneaked out saying that he would consult with leaders of the sect regarding those matters which he could not refute.[4]

It was also during those earlier years that Augustine wrote the treatise *On Two Souls*, in which he attempted to refute the Manichaean notion

---

[3]*On the Usefulness of Believing* 8.20.
[4]Posidius, *Life of Saint Augustine* 6.

that there are in a human being two souls, one spiritual and of light, and the other material and of darkness. In order to refute the attacks of Manichaeans who claimed that they based their doctrines purely on reason, without having recourse to other authorities, he wrote the beautiful short work *On the Usefulness of Believing*. Since one of the favorite subjects of the Manichaeans was that the God of the Old Testament is not the same as the God of Jesus but rather an inferior being, and that therefore the New Testament contradicts the Old, Augustine wrote several works trying to prove exactly the opposite. One of the first was *Against Adiamantus*, written in about 395. Adiamantus had been one of the main followers and proponents of the teachings of Mani. In secret documents the Manichaeans offered numerous differences and contradictions between the Old and the New Testaments. Augustine wrote a detailed refutation of many of these apparent contradictions. He would later say that there were so many that he had not been able to discuss them all in this particular work, although he certainly had done it at various times from the pulpit. With the same purpose in mind he wrote *On Genesis to the Letter*, an extensive work that he began in 401 and did not finish until 415.

Since the Manichaeans held that light cannot do evil and darkness cannot do good, in 388 Augustine began composing *On Free Will*, a book he did not complete until 395. In 393 he began refuting a writing of Mani in his *Against an Epistle of the Manicheans*, and he completed this work three years later.

Although as time went by Augustine had to turn his attention mostly to the Donatists and Pelagians—movements that will be discussed in the next two chapters—Augustine continued writing against the Manichaeans works such as *On the Nature of the Good* (year 405). He also continued debating Manichaean leaders. Among many such debates, Posidius tells us of one that took place in the year 404 with remarkable success.

> He also debated publicly with a certain Felix, one of the "elect," in the church in Hippo with great attendance, with a notarized record being kept. After the second or third discussion, after the error and vacuity of his sect had been shown, that Manichean converted to our holy faith and church, as may be seen in the acts of that event.[5]

---

[5]Posidius, *Life of Saint Augustine* 16.

The Manichaeans and Augustine's Thought

As we have seen, one of the great obstacles keeping Augustine from his mother's faith was the question of the origin and existence of evil. If God is good, powerful and maker of all that exists, how can one explain the existence of evil? For Augustine this was not merely the theoretical problem that is usually discussed under the heading of "theodicy," but was rather a profoundly personal matter, having to do with the evil he found within himself. He describes this struggle as follows:

> But then I was forced to ask further, "Who made me? Was it not my God, who is not merely good, but Goodness itself? . . . Is it in me simply so that I should deserve the punishment I suffer? Who established that ability in me, who planted in me this bitter cutting, when my whole being is from my most sweet God? If the devil is responsible, where did the devil come from? If he was a good angel who was transformed into a devil by his own perverted will, what was the origin of this evil will in him that turned him into a devil, when an angel is made entirely by the supremely good creator?"[6]

The question of the existence of evil may be posed at two different levels. The first and more theoretical is how to explain that a good God has created bad things. The second, more existential, is how to explain the inclination toward evil that is so deeply rooted in the soul. The Manichaeans seemed able to answer both questions. The existence of evil in the world is due to the fact that the world is not the creation of a single good god, but is rather the admixture of two principles that are equally powerful and eternal. This means that the existence of evil is simply the manifestation of the principle of evil or of darkness that is everywhere. And when it comes to the evil that resides in the will, this can be explained by asserting that, just as in the world there are two principles, there are two souls, one good and one evil. The inner struggle that a human being experiences is simply the conflict between these two souls. There is in each of us a good principle of light and also an evil one of darkness.

---

[6]*Confessions* 7.4.5. NCP I/1:162.

However, the Christian claim that there is a single God, creator of all things, makes the matter more difficult. Even if one were to presuppose that God has made the world from a preexistent matter, and that evil is the result of that matter, this does not resolve the question. If God did create the world out of evil matter, one may still ask why God couldn't transform that matter, and whether he actually wished to do so.

> So where does it come from, if the good God made all things good? He is the greatest good, to be sure, the supreme good, and the things he has made are lesser goods; nonetheless creator and creatures are all good. Whence, then, comes evil? Was something bad in the material he used, so that though he formed it and disposed it in order he left in it some element that was not turned to good? But why? Did he lack the power so to convert and change it all so that no evil would remain, he who is omnipotent? In any case, why would he have chosen to use it for making things, rather than using this same almighty power to destroy it entirely?[7]

Once again, Augustine did not approach this issue as a matter of mere curiosity or philosophical disquisition, but as one that caused him profound restlessness and anguish. As he himself would say, "What agonizing birth-pangs tore my heart, what groans it uttered, O my God!"[8]

Those who proved most helpful in pulling Augustine out of this anguishing perplexity were not Christian theologians, nor even his mother, Monica, but the Neoplatonic philosophers. Neoplatonism was a radical monism that held that there is ultimately only one reality, the ineffable One. From that reality proceeds every other reality, just as a stone dropping into the water causes a series of concentric circles. And just as in those circles the force of the initial impact is diluted as the circles widen and become more distant, thus also in the case of the single reality; its beauty, goodness and power are diluted as it departs from the One, from which all reality comes. The entire world is nothing but a series of emanations from the One, all of them good, but some better than others according to how close they are to the One, from which they come and

---

[7]*Confessions* 7.6.7. NCP I/1:164.
[8]*Confessions* 7.7.11. NCP I/1:168.

to which they will all return. We have already seen the example of a monkey, which is not ugly in itself but is ugly if compared with higher beauty such as that of humans or angels. Again, there is nothing that is evil in itself, in its own substance.

This led Augustine to the conclusion that there is no such a thing as an evil substance. Even evil has no substance, but is rather the disorder that is produced when things depart from the ineffable One, creator of all things: "I inquired then what villainy might be, but I found no substance, only the perversity of a will twisted away from you, God, the supreme substance, toward the depths—a will that throws away its life within and swells with vanity abroad."[9]

Even though evil has no substance, this does not make it any less real. Certainly not so for Augustine, who was deeply concerned about the evil that he found within himself. The story about the stolen pears was not just a shameful memory of youthful mischief, but also a strong indication that the will of Augustine himself was corrupted. Thus, although Augustine could well say that evil was not a substance, he still knew that it was deeply rooted within his soul.

As we have seen, the manner in which Manichaeans solved the matter of evil within an individual was the same as the way they solved the problem of evil in the world: just as there are in the world two principles, one of light and one of darkness, there are also in a human being two souls, one good and another evil. Augustine summarizes the Manichaean doctrine by saying that they "claim that in a single body there are two souls; one divine which is in its nature like God, and another coming from the root of evil, which the good soul did not beget, nor produce."[10] And just as Augustine responds to the matter of evil by means of the absolute monism of Neoplatonism, he now responds to the matter of evil within himself by means of a radical affirmation of the unity of the soul. The struggle that takes place within the soul, constantly debating between good and evil, is not a conflict between two souls or two principles, but rather a difficult struggle that takes place within a single being, a

[9]*Confessions* 7.16.22. NCP I/1:176.
[10]*On True Religion* 9.16.

single soul: "Why is this not rather a sign of one soul, which can be carried to one side and then to the other by free will? For, when it happens to me, I see that my one self considers both and chooses one of them. But generally the one is attractive and the other is right, and, placed between them, we waver back and forth."[11]

In order to explain how this works, Augustine takes into account the force of habit, which may work for good as well as for evil. Past similar evil actions slowly create a habit in the soul, and that habit is strengthened by the mysterious manner in which the soul tends to forget the negative or painful aspects of past evil and only remembers their pleasure. This then becomes customary, so that the soul, as if by a habit, leans toward evil. But in the opposite direction it is also possible to create in the soul the habit of virtue, so that a correct decision becomes easier—although it is important to note that as years went by and Augustine had to continue dealing with his own imperfection as well as with pastoral issues, and particularly as a result of his debates with the Pelagians, Augustine became increasingly pessimistic as to the possible reach of such positive habits.

In brief, one of the main points at which Augustine's Manichaean experience and his interest in refuting the doctrines he had learned from them shows throughout his thought is his insistence on unity over against Manichaean dualism: the unity of God, the unity of creation, the unity of a human being and the unity between the two Testaments. In trying to underscore that unity, he found Neoplatonism quite helpful. However, as years went by Augustine began discovering the difference between that monism and the Christian doctrine of creation, in which God creates new beings that, even though they are the result of divine action, neither are divine nor partake of the divine nature. This, which is true of all created beings, has to be stressed above all when it comes to the case of the soul. Even though the soul may be the one reality among all those we know that is closest to God, it still is not divine.

> Let the soul acknowledge its condition; it isn't God. When the soul thinks it is God, it offends God; it finds in him a bringer, not of salvation, but of

---

[11] *The Two Souls* 13.19. NCP I/11:131.

condemnation. Because when God condemns bad souls, he doesn't condemn himself; if, though, the soul is the same as what God is, he does condemn himself. . . . You cannot be your own light; you can't, you simply can't. . . . We are in need of enlightenment, we are not the light.[12]

In this entire process, seeing the need to reject Manichaean predeterminism, which claimed that the souls of light are predestined by their very nature to return to the reign of light and that the opposite is true of the souls of darkness, Augustine wrote extensively and strongly in favor of free will. This may surprise those of us who have repeatedly heard that Augustine is one of the main proponents of the doctrine of predestination.

While Augustine is frequently presented as the great teacher of predestination, and this is true, he also defended free will. This may be seen particularly in his treatise *On Free Will*, which Augustine began writing in Rome and did not complete until several years later in Hippo. Thus this treatise is not just his first reaction against Manichaeism but also a carefully formulated view that Augustine never abandoned.

The treatise takes the shape of a dialogue with his friend Evodius, who would later become a bishop. At the very beginning, Evodius asks: "Please tell me, can God be the author of evil?" Augustine's response begins with the distinction between two sorts of evil, for it is not the same when we say that someone has done an evil thing as when we say that someone has suffered some evil. In the first sense, Augustine is clear that God cannot do any such evil. But in the second sense, God does punish the wicked, and for them such punishment is evil. Thus only in that limited sense can one say that evil comes from God. However, this is not an absolute evil, but rather one that is such only from the limited perspective of the wicked, for the fact that God punishes them is not a true evil, but actually good. What Augustine proposes to discuss in this dialogue is not evil in this second sense, referring to that which displeases or pains us, but rather evil in the strict sense, which denotes that which is done against the commandments of God. (Note that in all of this Augustine is not discussing natural evil such as earthquakes, floods

---

[12]*Sermon* 182.4-5. NCP III/5:333-34.

or droughts. In other words, although the subject is the nature of evil, this is limited only to moral evil and its consequences. The wider subject of "theodicy"—how it can be that a good God permits such calamities—is not within the purview of this treatise. In general, when it comes to this other subject, Augustine seems to agree with the view of earlier theologians in North Africa, that the world is aging, and that just as our own aging causes pain and difficulty, so does the aging of the world bring about natural calamities.)

The question then is: How can a good and almighty God allow creatures—humans as well as angels—to do evil? Evodius puts it as follows: "I am still perplexed by the following: If sin comes from souls that were created by God and that come from God, how are we not to make God responsible for sin, since there is such a close relationship between God and the sinful soul?"[13]

In his understanding of what proper behavior is, Augustine was profoundly influenced both by Neoplatonism and by Stoicism, both of which claimed that good behavior is that which is led by reason. What opposes it is passion. Augustine did not believe that passions were evil, but he did believe that they make it difficult to follow the dictates of reason. Whether one does what reason commands or what passion dictates is a matter of one's free will: "The only thing that can lead the mind to follow its passions is its own free will."[14] In other words, an evil action is the result of free will, which opts for behavior suggested by passion and not by the rational principles that God has implanted in the human mind.

Although this explains how evil may originate in the human will, it still does not explain how it can be that the creator is not responsible for the evil performed by creatures, since free will itself is God's creation. Evodius summarizes the argument to this point and restates the problem as follows:

It seems to me that the matter of the origin of evil has been solved and clarified, as well as the nature of evil actions themselves. If I am not mistaken,

---

[13]*On Free Will* 1.2.4.
[14]*On Free Will* 1.9.21.

as has been argued, evil has its origin in the free decision of the will. But I still ask you whether the very will of which we are speaking and from which there is no doubt that sin originates, can be actually given to us by the one who made us. It would seem certain had we not been given such a will we would not have sinned, and it would therefore seem that God is the final author of our sin.[15]

Responding to this question, Augustine insists that all that exists is good, for to say that there are creatures that are by nature evil would lead to the dualism of the Manichaeans. But at the same time he distinguishes three sorts of goods: the higher, the intermediate and the lower.

> Therefore, virtues which allow us to live righteously, belong to the category of the higher goods. The various sorts of bodies, which are not necessary to live righteously, are among the lower. And the powers of the soul, without which it is impossible to live righteously, are intermediate goods. It is impossible to use virtues for evil. Of the other two kinds of goods, that is, the intermediate and the lesser, it is possible to use well, but also to abuse.[16]

The differences among these three levels of goods may be clarified with some examples. Higher goods include justice and love. It is impossible to use them for evil, as long as they are true justice and true love. Without love and justice there can be no virtue. Lesser goods are the members of the body. Correctly employed, the hand can do much good; but the same hand can also wound and kill. This does not mean that the hand itself is evil. What is evil is the use made of it—what Augustine calls "abuse." Furthermore, it is possible to live righteously without hands. Therefore a hand, which is one of the many goods created by God, should be useful for righteous living, but not necessary for it.

Between these two levels there is the intermediate good of free will. This is similar to the higher goods in that without it, it is impossible to live righteously. But it is also similar to the lesser goods in that it may be used for evil.

---

[15]*On Free Will* 1.16.35.
[16]*On Free Will* 2.19.51.

This intermediate good, free will, is what allows us both to choose between higher and lower goods and to determine the course of our actions. It is also what makes a human being worthy of praise or blame. Without it, our actions would be neither good nor evil, but simply natural. The movement of a stone that falls or of water that flows is natural, for the stone does not decide to fall nor the water to flow. They do such things by reason of their own nature. For a stone to fall does not make it worthy of praise or of blame. But when the will opts for the good this does make it worthy of praise. And if it opts for evil, it is worthy of censure. Likewise, that which we do by nature, and not out of a free decision, is neither praiseworthy nor evil. This is important, for if the will were simply the result of external forces it would not be free, and therefore there would be no merit or blame in any action. Outside forces may push us in one direction or the other; but eventually all that counts is the free decision of the will, even amid such pressures. As Augustine himself puts it, "What can be the cause of the will prior to the will itself? Either this cause is the will itself, which means that we have come to the root of what we seek, or it is not the will, and in that case the will does not sin."[17]

In brief, upon creating human beings God gave them this intermediate good that is free will. In itself, freedom is good and is part of the perfection of the human creature. But since it is an intermediate good, it may be used for evil.

There is still another problem that Evodius raises before Augustine. How can our actions be free if God already knows them? Evodius says: "I still do not see how these two things do not contradict one another: divine foreknowledge of our sins; and our own freedom to sin."[18] Augustine's answer is that God knows what we will decide, but does not determine it. This is similar to what happens with our own memory, which remembers many things even though they are things that one has chosen to do. We remember those events that we ourselves produced as well as others that happened for other reasons. Likewise, God knows both that which will happen because God has determined that it should be so and

---

[17]*On Free Will* 3.17.49.
[18]*On Free Will* 3.4.9.

that which will happen out of a free decision of God's creatures. This does not make those actions less free, just as our present knowledge of past decisions does not contradict their free nature.

Among the various controversies in which Augustine was involved, it was against Manichaeism that he was most successful—although the one that is most remembered and that has made greater impact on later theology was his controversy with Pelagianism. Manichaeism presented itself as a highly rational system that was able to explain all the mysteries and contradictions of the universe and of life. Therefore, refuting it by intellectual means would yield significant results. There are frequent reports of debates between Augustine and a Manichaean teacher in which Augustine was without any doubt the victor. Eventually, in great part thanks to the efforts and the writings of Augustine, Manichaeism disappeared from North Africa. When, years later, similar dualistic or Manichaean tendencies arose—as among the Bogomils and the Albigensians in the Middle Ages, or among some others that today follow speculations similar to those of the Manichaeans and Gnostics—the thought and writings of Augustine have provided abundant material to refute such tendencies.

However, although his polemics against the Manichaeans dominated the first years of Augustine's intellectual production, soon other debates would eclipse this one. The first was his controversy with the Donatists, to which we must now turn.

5

The Shepherd and
the Donatists

THE BACKGROUND

By the last decades of the third century, the northern shores of Africa were one of the regions in which Christianity grew most rapidly. In its early stages, that growth took place mostly in Carthage and in other centers of Roman culture and civilization. This should not surprise us, for the first Christian expansion took place among people who spoke Greek, and in Africa it was only the educated elite who knew this language. But soon believers among that educated elite began witnessing among their neighbors of Latin speech, and this is the reason why Christian theology in Latin had its origin—and almost all its main theologians until the fifth century—in North Africa.

From that Latin population, the gospel rapidly spread among the masses that still spoke the ancient African languages—some Punic, but the majority Berber or Libyan. It was among these masses that Christianity experienced an explosive growth, to the point that already at the beginning of the fourth century there were areas in which most of the population had become Christian. As is often the case in similar circumstances, this process of conversion was aided by the discontent of the masses with the exploitative Roman regime. The Roman system of collecting taxes, which simply made the authorities of each area responsible for meeting a certain quota, allowing them also to collect more than was required and keep the difference, led not only to corruption but also to onerous taxation of the lower classes, particularly of farmers with limited lands. The burden was such that many would simply abandon their lands, for they could not pay the taxes imposed on them.

A fairly common practice among those charged with collecting taxes was to offer loans to landholders so they could pay their taxes, and then take possession of the land when the farmer could not cover his debt. For these and similar reasons, throughout the area, but particularly among the poorer urban population and among the peasantry in the interior lands, Romans and their agents were profoundly disliked, and frequently had to be guarded by military escorts as they set out to collect taxes. Since these Romans who exploited and oppressed the people were also persecuting Christianity, soon many among the lower echelons of society began looking favorably on Christianity. Thus the rapid conversion of a good part of the area to Christianity also had undertones of protest, or at least of resistance against the existing order.

As already stated, the theological perspective that soon became dominant among Christians in Africa was moralistic in nature, seeing God above all as a legislator and judge who demanded obedience and holiness. From that perspective the main mark of the church is its holiness—not in the sense of having been chosen or established by God, but rather in the moral sense of being free of sin. Quite naturally, this perspective leads to repeated schisms, for there is always someone who is convinced that the church as it presently exists is not sufficiently holy and therefore will leave it in order to create another that is holier—although, as history has repeatedly shown, there will always be within that new church others who will demand even greater holiness, and will leave in order to create an even holier church.

It is also important to remember that the Roman understanding of authority differed from that of the traditional African population. For the Romans, authority resided in the office of a person, and not in that person's virtues. Naturally, it was at least theoretically expected that those in authority would be virtuous; but if they were not, this was no excuse not to obey them until they were deposed by higher authority. From the African perspective, authority would reside in the person rather than in the office. One became chief of a tribe or of a family because one was valiant, strong, wise, virtuous and so on. But if a chief turned out to be a coward or a fool, that very fact deprived him of his authority, and obedience was due to another chief who would be more valorous, strong or wise.

The consequences of all this may be seen in several episodes that took place in the African church before Augustine's time. Two of the most important examples should suffice. The first is the case of Montanism and its champion Tertullian. Montanism was a movement originating in Phrygia that declared that the existing church did not possess the Holy Spirit, who had come to rest now on Montanus and his followers. As proof of this, they offered their holiness, which they claimed was greater than that of the rest of Christians, and also their ecstatic experiences. Upon reaching Africa, Montanism soon achieved the conversion of Tertullian, who had become widely respected as the first Christian theologian writing in Latin. Tertullian embraced Montanism enthusiastically. The moral rigorism of Montanism in general and of Tertullian in particular may be seen in the manner in which he saw the historical development of faith. According to him, there was first the law of Moses; then came the "law of the gospel," which is stricter than that of Moses; and, finally, the "law of the Spirit," which is even stricter than the law of Jesus. The Montanists, who are holier because they follow the law of the Spirit, can then claim to be the true church. But the history of Tertullian himself shows the natural consequences of such rigoristic attitudes, for after being part of the Montanist church he decided that this was not sufficiently holy and withdrew from it—according to some ancient writers, creating the sect of the "Tertullianists."

The second example took place half a century later. At that point the bishop of Carthage was Cyprian, who to this day is considered one of the great leaders of the ancient church. When persecution broke out, Cyprian hid while others were taken before the authorities. Many among the latter were killed, but others remained in prison—sometimes suffering torture—until persecution abated. At that point they were given the title of "confessors," because they had confessed the faith in difficult times and at a high personal cost. As persecution passed, some among the "lapsed"—that is, those who had faltered at the threat of persecution—wanted to return to the bosom of the church. Cyprian was quite ready to allow such a thing, but insisted that it should be the properly established church authorities—including Cyprian himself—who should determine whom to restore to the community of the church, and under what conditions. But some of the lapsed would go before the confessors, who would absolve them of their sin and declare them to be back in communion with the church. In that conflict we may see two different ways of understanding authority. On the one hand, Cyprian, intellectually formed in Roman schooling, thought that it was bishops who had the authority to decide on the restoration of the lapsed. On the other hand, his opponents, mostly Africans, insisted that the confessors, by virtue of having proved the strength of their faith, were the ones who had authority regarding the restoration of the lapsed—and at the same time pointed out that Cyprian, who had hid at the threat of persecution, had less authority than they did.

THE ORIGINS OF DONATISM

These two elements—the holiness of the church and the contrast between a notion of authority as derived from office and another notion of authority as grounded in behavior—would play an important role in the rise of Donatism and in the debates surrounding it. Although the *Church History* of Eusebius of Caesarea does not say much on the matter because Eusebius did not have access to the records of what took place in Africa, it is clear from his work that the provinces of Africa and Numidia suffered greatly during the time of what came to be called the "great persecution" under Diocletian at the beginning of the fourth century. Those who yielded before imperial pressure were such that, according to an eyewitness, the pagan temples were overflowing. There were also numerous martyrs and—following the African traditions that have already been mentioned—they were given great authority and even magical powers. Thus, for instance, we are told of a rich woman by the name of Lucilla who had the bone of a martyr, which she kissed before partaking of Communion, as if the validity of Communion were due to the martyr rather than to Communion itself, or to the authority of the celebrant or of the congregation in the name of the whole church.

The more Romanized bishops of Carthage and the surrounding area held that before someone could be called a "martyr" it was necessary for the bishops to recognize that person as such. Not all the dead deserved that title. Much of the controversy had to do with the so-called spontaneous—people who had voluntarily offered themselves for martyrdom even before they were accused by the authorities. Were such people true martyrs? Was not martyrdom a "crown" for which God chose some and that therefore could not be wrested by an act of fanatical daring? Were not Christians supposed to flee from persecution, and to yield to martyrdom only when it became unavoidable? This had been debated for a long time, and generally the conclusion had been that the spontaneous were not true martyrs. But not all agreed on that point, and in the province of Africa and nearby areas there were always—at least since the time of Tertullian—those who held that the martyrdom of the spontaneous was valid. The case of Lucilla's bone is a sample of the conflicts this produced. No one knows the identity of the martyr whom Lucilla venerated; but it was clear that the authorities of the church had not declared him a martyr formally acknowledged—*vindicatus*. Thus the conflict between Lucilla and Caecilian, who eventually became bishop of Carthage, was not only grounded on the claim on the part of Caecilian—who at that point was an archdeacon—that Lucilla was superstitious but also on the fact that the martyr whom Lucilla venerated was not an acknowledged one. Here again we see the contrast between two understandings of authority. For Lucilla, the martyr had become such by virtue of his actions, and did not need ecclesiastical certification in order to be venerated. For Caecilian, since Lucilla's martyr was not *vindicatus*, he should not be honored as a martyr until the authorities of the church had acknowledged him.

Due to a series of political circumstances, persecution in Africa abated in 305, before it did so in other parts of the empire. Toward the end of 311, the bishop of Carthage died in a visit to Rome, and it was necessary to elect a successor. For more than half a century the custom had been established that the main bishop in Numidia, the province next to Pro-consular Africa, would participate in the consecration of his new col-league in Carthage. But, fearful that the Numidians would intervene in favor of a candidate of more extreme positions, the Carthaginians hurried to elect Caecilian, who as an archdeacon under the previous bishop had given indications that his policies would be moderate. Im-mediately, so as to not give time to the bishops of Numidia or other nearby regions in the interior of the land to express their disagreement, Caecilian was consecrated by three other bishops, two from the province of Africa and the third from the nearby province of Byzacena—which the Numidians took as a clear attempt to exclude them.

While Caecilian was supported by many of the Carthaginians of Roman culture, there were some who felt that his character was such that he should not have been made a bishop. One of the leaders of this op-position was Lucilla—perhaps seeking revenge for her humiliation years earlier when Caecilian had chastised her for her devotion to a martyr who had not been *vindicatus*. With her economic support, opposition increased, and then centered on the accusation that one of the three bishops who had consecrated Caecilian, Felix of Aphtunga, was among those who were now called *traditores*.

The pejorative title of *traditor* had arisen during the persecution. In that "great persecution" the main objective of the authorities was not to create martyrs—even though they did create quite a few—but rather to create apostates, particularly among the leaders, and thus weaken the church. Therefore the first imperial decree required that church buildings be destroyed and that bishops and any other leaders who had copies of the Christian Scriptures should turn them over to be burned. Later other edicts widened the scope of persecution, making it obligatory for all to worship the gods, and decreeing the death penalty for those who refused to do so. The responses to the edict requiring the surrendering of Scripture varied. Some simply refused to turn them over and suffered martyrdom or at least imprisonment and torture—in which case they became confessors. Others, knowing the ignorance of the authorities themselves, turned over heretical books or some other writings, claiming these to be Christian Scriptures. Many fled to remote areas, taking with them the sacred books, and remained there until persecution passed. And still others simply obeyed the imperial decree and turned over the sacred books to be destroyed by fire. These others were dubbed *traditores*—that is, "givers" or betrayers—for having given up the Scriptures.

What Caecilian's opposition then claimed was, first, that Felix was a *traditor*, and that in consequence he was not a true bishop and he did not have authority to consecrate Caecilian. Furthermore, they also claimed that since the other two bishops had joined Felix they had become contaminated by him. Thus, in essence, the debate now had to do mostly with the character and origin of authority and with holiness understood as purity. According to Caecilian and his followers, he had been validly consecrated, for the ceremony had taken place under the direction of three properly constituted bishops. For the opposition, if Felix was a *traditor* this deprived him of his episcopal authority. And if others joined him this contaminated them too, depriving them of their sanctity, and therefore of their authority as bishops. On the basis of such arguments, the opposition elected a rival bishop, whom the bishops of Numidia now consecrated. Since this man died soon, he was succeeded by Donatus of Casa Nigra, whose leadership was such that from then on the party received the name of "Donatists." Donatus was a man of firm conviction and apparently austere character, and was much admired even by his opponents. Given those traits he was able to claim for his party a greater holiness than their opponents. Even these opponents acknowledged his virtue. Augustine, who completely disagreed with his doctrines, called both him and Cyprian "precious gems."

The persecution ended and a new situation developed in which the imperial government, through the example of Constantine, seemed to favor Christians ever more. At the same time many among the Romanized Carthaginians began coming to church and requesting baptism. From the perspective of the poor urban population and of peasants—particularly in Numidia—who had embraced Christianity and held fast to it during persecution, this seemed a great apostasy. Until very recently, those impoverished folk had paid a high price for their faith. Now the same elite that was always running things was joining the church, and even claiming and obtaining privileges in it.

THE COURSE OF DONATISM

As a result, the schism began taking on ethnic and racial overtones, and soon was supported by the great majority of the population in Numidia and farther east, as well as by many in the interior of the province of Africa itself and even among the lower echelons of society in Carthage. While Augustine was alive, Jerome declared that Donatism had become the religion "of almost all of Africa." And Augustine says that in his own native town of Tagaste the population had become "totally Donatist" until imperial pressure began turning it in a different direction.

The news of the conflict between Caecilian and his opponents reached Emperor Constantine, who clearly took the side of Caecilian and his supporters—which is not surprising, since the emperor would not have much sympathy for the separatist tendencies of Donatism, particularly since he had hoped the church would become "the cement of the empire." At the same time, Caecilian was able to gather the recognition of the rest of the church, in Europe as well as in the Greek-speaking East, and therefore claimed that his party was "Catholic," while the Donatists were openly schismatic. This was confirmed by a synod of bishops proceeding from all over the Christian West—including even Great Britain—which gathered in Arles in 314. Finally, in 317, the emperor ordered that all Donatist churches be confiscated and that the leaders of the movement be sent into exile. But the Donatists would not obey, and Caecilian requested firmer action by the imperial authorities. This raised the conflict to a higher level. In Carthage and nearby there were riots and massacres. But in Numidia, Mauritania and other areas where Donatism was particularly strong the edicts of Constantine were not applied. As a consequence of all this, the rivalry and even hatred between the two sides increased, and the regionalist tendencies of Donatism became more marked. Finally, in 325, seeing that his policies did not seem to stop Donatism, Constantine rescinded his previous decrees and granted tolerance to Donatists.

From that point on Donatism grew rapidly. Soon Donatus was able to gather councils in which almost three hundred bishops attended. The "Catholic" party of Caecilian was practically reduced to a small group in Carthage and a few major cities. From then on, until 363, Donatism was dominant in all the provinces of Latin-speaking North Africa.

But these very triumphs brought new problems to Donatism. A movement that had originally grown among the masses now began making headway among the higher and more cultured elements of society, and much of the leadership passed on to them. These new leaders did not have the strong anti-imperial sentiments of the first Donatists and the lower classes, urban as well as rural. Soon many among the Donatists became discontent with this new leadership. Around the year 340, this resulted in a movement known as the Circumcellions, which resorted to violence against the Catholic party and sometimes even against some of the more moderate Donatist leaders. Circumcellions were particularly numerous in the interior of Numidia and in Mauritania, where the hostility to all things Roman was deep, and the Romans, at that time concerned over much more serious dangers in Europe, were not able to impose their authority. While the Circumcellions declared themselves Donatists, and on the basis of religious disagreement attacked and sacked the villas and properties of the Catholics, they were also a movement of social revolution that would even turn to terrorism in order to achieve its purposes—purposes that were in any case not well defined, but were rather limited to the desire to destroy everything Roman. The more moderate Donatists tried to distance themselves from the Circumcellions. But when they needed the support of the Circumcellions they would make use of it.

In 347 the Roman authorities intervened once again. Their support of the Catholic party was unavoidable, for this was the party that, besides being acknowledged as the true church by the rest of the church, was more sympathetic toward the state. As to Donatus, when authorities invited him to expound his arguments, he simply replied that "the emperor has nothing to do with the church." Under fierce pressure from the state, Donatism began waning, both in the city of Carthage and in the nearby province of Africa, while it was still strong in Numidia and Mauritania. In Carthage itself, the imperial legate decreed the reunion of the two churches under the direction of the Catholic bishop, and sent Donatus into an exile from which he never returned. Even in Rome there was now a small group that expressed Donatist tendencies, and who claimed that their own bishop in Rome, since he still held communion with some of the African *traditores*, was not a true bishop—which led them to propose a rival candidate. But this group in Rome was never large, as they gathered in caves in the mountains, their members came to be known as the Mountaineers. In the provinces of Africa, Numidia and Mauritania, persecution of Donatists became ever more violent and cruel.

This persecution stopped suddenly when Julian—commonly known as "the Apostate"—attained the imperial throne. Julian wished to restore paganism, and therefore he was very pleased by the growing disagreements and conflicts among Christians. He soon decreed that the properties of Donatist churches that had been confiscated were to be returned, and that there would no longer be any pressure against Donatism. Once again, Donatism became dominant in the provinces Numidia and Mauritania, although no longer in Africa itself. This also provided an opportunity for the development of remarkable leaders among the Donatists, who did much for the prestige of the movement. The most distinguished among them was Tyconius, from whom, as we shall see in another chapter, Augustine took some of the ideas that we now find in his great opus, the *City of God*.

When Julian died the persecution against the Donatists returned, while the activities of the Circumcellions increased in scope as well as in violence. In the face of persecution, the main Donatist leaders openly declared that they favored the use of force, coming to the point of declaring that it was legitimate to use violence in opposition to the authorities that persecuted them and also against the church that was supported by those authorities. This in turn led to another schism in the long series of divisions within Donatism. The new group, called Rogatists after their leader Rogatus, insisted on abstaining from all violence as part of the holiness that was required of the true church and its members. When in Mauritania and the neighboring areas a certain Firmius rebelled against Roman power and took the title of king, the Donatists supported him and proclaimed him the legitimate emperor, rather than the one from Rome. When that rebellion failed, once again the Donatists suffered the weight of imperial authority and revenge. Two decades later history seemed to repeat itself, for a brother of Firmius by the name of Gildo directed a new rebellion and also sought the support of the Donatists and Circumcellions. When finally the new rebellion was suppressed in 398, Donatism lost all political ascendency, and found itself under constant and growing pressure from the civil authorities. At the same time, since Donatism claimed to be the true church by being holier than its rival, it itself was divided by a multitude of schisms in which each claimed to be holier than the others—Rogatists, Maximinianists, Urbanists, Claudianists and so on.

AUGUSTINE'S THEOLOGICAL INTERVENTION

Seven years before the suppression of Gildo's rebellion, Augustine had been ordained as a presbytery by Valerius. As a result, his writings and his intellectual labor took new directions. Up to that point, most of his concerns had been philosophical in nature, as may be seen in his earlier writings. He had only participated actively in the controversy with the Manichaeans, partly because many friends and acquaintances of his earlier life belonged to that sect, and partly because he himself had been a Manichaean and therefore felt a particular call to refute the beliefs that he had held before, and to lead to truth those whom before he had affirmed in error. But now, after his ordination, Augustine began focusing more attention on the controversies among Christians, and particularly on the need to refute Donatism. It is interesting to note that, although some among his own family were still Donatists, Augustine does not even mention Donatism in any of his writings before his ordination. In the entire narrative of the *Confessions* about his youth in Tagaste, he never says who among his friends and companions were Donatists and who were Catholic. It is quite probable that, since they were being persecuted, many of those who still held to Donatism did so secretly. Furthermore, even though these were times of great political unrest and even rebellions, of persecution and of violence, apparently the circles in which Augustine moved tried to stay away from such matters. As he says, after being ordained as a presbyter in Hippo he was frequently called to mediate in disputes in which Catholics as well as Donatists came to ask his opinion, and in Hippo itself there were families whose members, while belonging to different religious groups, were able to live under the same roof without great disruption. Apparently, in the north of Numidia, from Tagaste to Hippo, conflicts between Catholics and Donatists were not as bitter or as violent as in the rest of the province. Even though Augustine does not give details, it is clear that among his Berber relatives there were Donatists. In Tagaste practically all the population had been Donatists until a short time before the birth of Augustine, when finally imperial pressure led many Donatists to leave town, and others to embrace Catholicism. (Was Monica among the latter? Was her marriage to a Roman official what led her to abandon the Donatism that Roman authorities were persecuting? It is impossible to know.)

During the first years of his episcopacy, Augustine wrote several works against Donatism. In them he discusses mostly historical and theological issues, but does not seem to be aware that the issue was also social and cultural. Furthermore, on this particular point Augustine's thought does not seem ever to have come to grips with the social and emotional roots of Donatism, nor with the reason why theological and historical refutations were not enough to stop it. But in spite of that Augustine opposed Donatism on two fronts: one, that of theology and debate; and the other, that of politics, seeking the support of the state against Donatism. Therefore, in the present section of this chapter we shall focus mostly on his writings against Donatists and his debates with them, in order then, in the next section, to deal briefly with his political activities and the later course of Donatism.

One of Augustine's earliest writings against the Donatists (possibly written in 393) was his *Psalm Against the Opinion of Donatus*, a poetical composition in which he summarized, repeated and popularized the arguments that had been employed by Optatus of Milevis—the only author who at that time had written in some detail of the history of the schism and sought to refute Donatism. Augustine's psalm had twenty stanzas of twelve verses each. Since each stanza began with one of the letters of the alphabet, this poem has also been known as *Augustine's ABC*. It is clear from this book that Augustine understood quite well that Donatism was a mass movement, and that in order to combat it, it was necessary to reach the common people. When he became a bishop in 395, Augustine began a series of lectures and debates with various Donatist leaders, as well as abundant correspondence with them. That correspondence shows him dealing respectfully with the Donatist leaders, for his purpose was not to defeat his readers but to convince them. In 400, he wrote a work in three books, *Against the Epistle of Parmenium*. The recently deceased Donatist bishop of Carthage had published a letter in which he criticized the moderate Donatist Tyconius, who had considered that those who opposed Donatism were correct in insisting that the church has to be universal and cannot be limited to the coast of Africa. Augustine, while disagreeing with Tyconius on other points, defends him, arguing that in truth Donatism, by the very fact of being limited to a particular region, cannot claim to be "catholic." Later in his *Seven Books on Baptism*, he would repeat and amplify an argument that Optatus had employed before, that the efficacy of a sacrament does not depend on the holiness of the celebrant. Against Petulian, who at that point was the main spokesman for Donatism, he wrote two books, and then a third one. Petulian responded to the first two. At about the same time he wrote *On the Unity of the Church*, a treatise debating the various Donatist theses. To the list may be added several minor works, some of which have been lost, as well as numerous sermons and letters. As the controversy advanced, the tone on both sides became less respectful and more virulent.

The arguments of Augustine in these writings are mostly historical and theological. The historical arguments are of less importance for the later history of Christianity, for Augustine simply denies the Donatist claim that Caecilian had been consecrated by a *traditor*, and then offers a number of cases of Donatists who he claims were *traditores*.

His theological arguments are much more significant, for their imprint on Christian theology may be seen even to this day.

It is clear that the main subject of disagreement between Augustine and the Donatists was the nature of the church. According to the Donatists, the holiness of the church required that its members be holy, and therefore it was necessary to exclude from it the original *traditores* as well as any other person related to them. Then, as a consequence of the debate on the holiness of the church and of those holding authority within it, the question arose about the character and validity of sacraments. The initial argument of the Donatists was that the ordination of Caecilian had not been valid because bishops who had been *traditores* took part in it, and that as a consequence all the sacraments offered by Caecilian as well as by anyone else who was in communion with him were invalid.

By Augustine's time another issue had been added to the debate, now having to do with the intervention of imperial forces persecuting Donatism: Is such an intervention valid? What criteria may justify the use of force and even of violence? Thus the three main themes in Augustine's polemic against the Donatists are the nature of the church, the validity of sacraments and the justification of violence—usually called the "just war theory."

The nature of the church, and particularly its holiness, had been a concern among North African Christians from a long time before Augustine. In the third century, Cyprian had insisted that it is impossible in this world to distinguish between the wheat and the chaff, and that there would always be, hidden within the holy wheat of the church, the chaff planted by the evil one. Augustine echoes Cyprian in this point, refuting those who believe that the church is holy because its members are holy: "Regarding chaff that has been mixed in with the planting of the wheat, the Lord says: 'Allow both to grow until the harvest.'"[1] Likewise, in a sermon he calls his audience to be aware

> that there are in the Church both good and bad people, whom we often call grain and chaff. None should desert the threshing floor before the

---

[1] *On the Unity of the Church* 14.35.

time; they should put up with the chaff during threshing, they should put up with it on the threshing floor. After all, there won't be any to put up with in the barn. The winnower is coming, who will divide the bad from the good. There will also be a material separation, now preceded by a spiritual one. Always be disconnected from bad people in your hearts; for the time being be cautiously connected with them socially in the body.[2]

In response to the Donatist claim that they are the true church due to their own holiness, Augustine first of all adduces the empirical proof that even among the Donatists there are those who are far from saintly. It is not only a matter of the heedless violence of the Circumcellions, but also of drunkenness, lying, fornication and many of the other vices that abound in the world being also present among the more moderate Donatists. Furthermore, even were they holy in all these things, they would still not be holy for the very reason that they are schismatics, for schism itself is a lack of love, and without love there is no holiness. Thus in purely empirical terms it is shown that if the church were to subsist by virtue of the holiness of its members, it would have ceased a long time ago, for since the very beginning there were in the church both wheat and tares, and even Judas partook of the Last Supper.

What makes the church holy is not its members, but its head, Jesus Christ. Under that head, and as part of his body, the faithful seek to live in holiness, even while knowing that they cannot be truly freed from the stain of Adam's sin, of which all humanity partakes. But mixed among the wheat of the truly faithful there is also the chaff or straw of the impious, and the two will not be separated before the Day of Judgment.

Meanwhile, it is helpful to think of the difference between the invisible church and the visible. The latter is composed of all those who call themselves Christians, no matter whether they are really such or not. In the visible church, as in the field of the parable or in the threshing floor, wheat is mixed with tares or chaff. And although there might be some indications as to who belongs to one category or the other, we cannot now distinguish absolutely between them, but must await the Day of

---

[2]*Sermon* 88.19. NCP III/3:431.

Judgment. Until then, within the visible church there will be faithful believers as well as hypocrites, true Christians and others who are not. In contrast with the visible church, but within it, there is the invisible church. This is the body of Christ, the totality of those who are to be saved—or, as Augustine will say later, of the elect. But this contrast is not such that it is possible to be part of the invisible church while abandoning the visible. Whoever leaves the visible church claiming a greater holiness is also withdrawing from the invisible church, from the one and only body of Christ. It is important to underscore this point, for in later times the distinction between the visible and the invisible church has been used to claim that, after all, there is no need to belong to the church visible. Augustine would never agree. For him, the invisible church exists only within the visible, and therefore the latter is not to be cast aside, in spite of the tares that may be growing within it.

The holiness of the church is to be affirmed only about the invisible church, about the totality of those members who, joined to the Head, are part of the body of Christ. But since this invisible church exists only within the visible, the latter is due the respect and love of every believer, and withdrawing from it is a lack of love and is the same as withdrawing from the invisible church and therefore from Jesus Christ himself.

This church that is holy by virtue of Jesus Christ is one by virtue of its union with him, and is also "catholic" by virtue of its presence throughout the world. Augustine sees the catholicity of the church as consisting precisely in that presence. This was a very useful argument in his controversy against the Donatists, for their movement was centered in Africa and had very few followers elsewhere. According to Augustine, the true church is "catholic" because it is universal. And here once again we see the indissoluble link—that is, indissoluble until the Day of Judgment—between the visible and the invisible church. Naturally, the church whose presence may be seen in all parts of the world is the visible. But that visible presence is a sign of the presence of the invisible church within it.

It is due to the importance of this visible church that unity is so important. And it is also for the same reason that the authorities that have been established by that visible church are not to be despised. Augustine knew of and in one of his letters gave witness to a line of succession that supposedly connected the bishops of Rome with Saint Peter. But that order of succession did not mean that all the bishops of Rome were holy or perfect, as would have to be the case if the holiness of the church depended on the holiness of its members or of its leaders. On the contrary, Augustine says:

> Even if during those times some traditor crept into the order of bishops that runs from Peter himself to Anastasius, who now occupies that see, it would not bring any harm to the Church or to the innocent Christians, to whom the Lord in his foresight said concerning bad superiors, *Do what they say, but do not do what they do. For they speak, but they do not act accordingly* (Mt 23:3). He said this in order that the hope of the believer might be certain and that such hope, not placed in a human being, but in the Lord, would not be blown away by the storm of sacrilegious schism, as these Donatists are blown away.[3]

In this entire argument Augustine is adhering to the traditional Roman view of authority, over against the manner in which the ancient African tradition understood it. As has been stated, the Romans did not believe that authority resided in the person as such or in that person's character, but rather in the office. Whoever is appointed as a governor has the authority to govern, no matter how corrupt he may be, until he is deposed by higher authority. By contrast, among the Libyans or Berbers authority resided in the person's nature itself and character, and the office was the result of that authority, not vice versa. Thus, by declaring that the bishop of Rome, even if he might have been a *traditor*, would not lose his authority, Augustine is affirming the Roman side of his own identity, preferring it over the Berber.

It is in this visible church and under its authority that the sacraments are celebrated. In Augustine's time it was still not determined how many sacraments there were—a process that would not be completed until the twelfth and thirteenth centuries—and therefore when speaking of sacraments Augustine refers to several rites and religious practices. For our purposes, our

---

[3]*Letter* 53.1.3. NCP II/1:205.

interest will focus on the rites of ordination, baptism and Communion, and on the validity and efficacy of such rites. This was of great importance for Augustine, for this was precisely the core issue at which he differed from the Donatists. The schism had arisen out of the claim by the Donatists that a bishop who was a *traditor* had been part of Caecilian's ordination and that, since that bishop was unworthy, the ordination itself was not valid. In consequence, any ordination by Caecilian or those who supported him—every ordination that was not carried out by the Donatists themselves—was invalid. Following this same line of argument, equally invalid were baptism and Communion celebrated by any who did not belong to the supposedly pure line of succession of the Donatists.

This aspect of the controversy had been foreshadowed in the third century, when Cyprian, the bishop of Carthage, clashed with Stephen, his counterpart in Rome. What was then being debated was whether or not a baptism received from heretical hands was valid, or whether heretics converted to the orthodox faith had to be rebaptized. Accepting such baptism received from heretics was common practice in Rome and throughout much of the church, but certainly not in Africa, where it was customary to rebaptize converted heretics. The conflict almost led to a breach between Rome and Carthage, and this was avoided only because both Stephen and Cyprian died. Although for some time the North Africans continued rebaptizing converted heretics, such practice was slowly abandoned, so that already before the time of Augustine those baptized by heretics were considered legitimately baptized.

All of this came to the surface once again during the Donatist schism. The Donatists, claiming the authority of Cyprian, insisted that baptism, as well as any other rite, celebrated by unworthy ministers was not valid. Thus, although Augustine defended the common practice of accepting baptism as well as other rites celebrated by the Donatists, the latter insisted on the need to rebaptize Catholics who joined the Donatist ranks. The reasons for such a policy were the same ones leading the Donatists to declare that the ordination of Caecilian was void, and that so were all other rites celebrated by him and his followers—including baptism and Communion.

In this entire argument, Augustine could make use of the arguments proposed by Bishop Optatus of Milevis, who had written the work *Seven Books Against the Donatists*. There he had insisted on the validity of baptism received from heretical hands, for in the act of baptism "the One who does the washing is not the human being, but God." He had also declared that "if you offer another baptism, you offer another faith; if you offer another faith, you offer another Christ; and if you offer another Christ, you offer another God."[4] Following this same argument, Augustine points out that if, as the Donatists claim, the validity of baptism depends on the merits of the one celebrating it, then

> there will have to be as many different degrees of baptism as there are different degrees of merit, and each one will believe that they are receiving something better than the rest. But this is not what happens, for everyone who is baptized receives the same baptism and the same power: In fact, if the holiness of baptism varies according to the diversity of merits, there will be as many variations in baptism as there are variations in merit; and the better the person one is baptized by seems to be, the better the baptism one will be thought to have received. . . . So then, when a good man baptizes and a better man baptizes, it does not mean that this person receives something good, that person something better; but although one of the ministers was good and the other better, what was received was one and the same, not something better in this person, inferior in that one. So too, when a bad person baptizes, with the church either not knowing what he is like or tolerating it.[5]

In other words, the validity, efficacy or virtue of baptism does not depend on the one who administers it, for baptism itself is an act of God. Much later, in the thirteenth century, Peter of Poitiers expressed this point by distinguishing between two phrases that have become classical: *ex opere operato* (by action of the act itself) and *ex opere operantis* (by action of the one acting). The validity of baptism is not *ex opere operantis* but rather *ex opera operato*—that is, it is not the result of the one administering it, but is the result of baptism itself and of the God whose power stands behind it.

---

[4]*On the Donatist Schism* 5.4.
[5]*Homilies on the Gospel of John* 6.8. NCP I/12:127-28.

A third important point at which the controversy of Augustine with the Donatists left an imprint in the later course of church history, besides those that have been discussed having to do with ecclesiology and the doctrine of the sacraments, is the theory of just war. Following the teachings of Jesus, the early Christians were pacifists, and it was not even allowed to baptize soldiers. But this attitude changed slowly, to the point that the number of members of the church among the military increased significantly. When, by action of Constantine and his successors, the empire declared itself to be Christian, the church had to face the question of the relationship between the Christian faith and the need to keep order and defend the borders in the face of the ever-increasing Germanic invasions. This may be seen in the case of Ambrose, the bishop of Milan who had such an important role in Augustine's conversion. When he was elected bishop of Milan, Ambrose had not even been baptized because, being a high government official, he would find himself having to make use of military power, as well as the authority of the police, and a baptized Christian should avoid all forms of violence. But when he became a bishop and saw his flock suffer under the chaos brought about by Germanic invasions, he found it necessary to affirm the use of military force by the state and to limit his pacifism to interpersonal relations and to the clergy, who were not to take arms. To that end, Ambrose made use of what had been said earlier by classical Greek and Latin writers—particularly Plato and Cicero— regarding the justification of war. This led to the beginning of a Christian theory of "just war," which Augustine would then develop, not only now to justify defense against foreign invasions, but also to justify the suppression of the Circumcellions by means of military action.

According to Augustine, for a war to be just the first requirement is that its purpose be peace. Writing to General Boniface, who had doubts about the use of military force, Augustine says that "we do not seek peace in order to stir up war, but we wage war in order to acquire peace."[6] The goal of every believer, as well as of the church and of a Christian state, must be to promote peace, and particularly to restore a peace that has

---

[6]*Letter* 189.6. NCP II/3:261.

been lost to violence and injustice. It is this that justifies military action against the Circumcellions, whose violence destroys peace. For the same reason, wars of conquest are not justified, for their purpose is not to restore peace but rather to extend the power of the conquerors. In the case of the Circumcellions, there was not such an element of conquest, for the area where the action was taking place was already part of the Roman Empire. And in the case of the Germanic peoples, their invasion of Roman territory was not justified, for it was a war of conquest. (Augustine was not aware that the Germanic peoples themselves were fleeing from other conquerors from the East.)

Second, a war can be just only if it is led by established authority—in which Augustine shows once again his respect for the Roman emphasis on authority not so much as a matter of personal merit, but of office. Were it not so, any individual or group of individuals could declare war on their neighbors, and private vengeance would be justified. Private violence is never justified, for only established authorities have the right to establish peace by means of punishment and even war.

Third, the war itself must be conducted in a just manner. Unnecessary violence against noncombatants, destruction of property, sacking and massacres can never be part of a just war.

And fourth—which is probably what a modern reader would find most surprising—war must be waged in an attitude of love. The purpose of war is not to destroy the enemy, but to lead it along the proper path.

> But we also have to do many things, even against the will of people who need to be punished with a certain kind of harshness, for we have to consider their benefit rather than their will. . . . For in rebuking a child, no matter how harshly, a father's love is surely never lost; he nonetheless does what the son does not want and causes pain to the son who, despite his unwillingness, he judges must be healed by pain. And for this reason, if this earthly state keeps the Christian commandments, even wars will not be waged without goodwill in order more easily to take into account the interests of the conquered with a view to a society made peaceful with piety and justice.[7]

---

[7]*Letter* 138.2.14. NCP II/3:232-33.

This entire theory of just war, which Augustine elaborated mostly to deal with the suppression of the Circumcellions but also in response to the Germanic invasions, became the doctrine most generally held among Christians, and to this day serves as a foundation for many discussions regarding Christian attitudes toward war and peace.

THE ROLE OF POLITICS

The context for all of this was the political and military process whereby imperial authorities sought to suppress Donatism, particularly in its more extreme expressions. The defeat in 398 of Gildo's rebellion, which many Donatists and practically all Circumcellions had supported, brought about ever-increasing difficulties for Donatism, as well as advantages for the Catholic party. Although there was violence on both sides, usually governmental pressure did not reach the point of the death penalty but rather was economic in nature. For instance, Donatists were not allowed to leave an inheritance. This led many among them to abandon their church and embrace the Catholic faith. Three years after Gildo's defeat, there were so many such conversions that the Catholic bishops of Africa, gathered in a synod, decided that, even though the accepted practice was that clergy converted from Donatism would become part of the laity, in those cases in which there were not sufficient clergy for the number of believers, each bishop should be free to determine the best policy. Soon what at first was allowed in exceptional cases became common practice, so that Donatist clergy who converted to the Catholic party would retain their former rank in their new faith community.

The same synod resolved to send missionaries to areas where the Donatists were predominant. As was to be expected, some of these missionaries suffered violence at the hands of the Circumcellions. Several of them, as well as other Catholic leaders, were kidnapped, beaten and tortured. In reaction to that situation, the Catholic party began to take hostages from among the Donatist leaders, and called on the Roman proconsul to provide protection and support. The proconsul convoked both sides to a series of debates and conferences. But the Donatists, fearing that the proconsul had already made a decision favoring the Catholic party, would not attend. Posidius, a colleague of Augustine, fell into a Circumcellion ambush and was barely able to escape alive. This led to a long suit that eventually was decided in favor of the Catholic party. Although this party was content with the verdict, they requested that the penalty not be applied, for Augustine and his colleagues wished to avoid the production of new "martyrs" whose sufferings would then inspire other Donatists.

Even so, Circumcellion violence continued to increase. The time came when Augustine and his companions could not feel safe outside the city of Hippo. A synod gathered in Carthage in 404 appealed to Roman authorities, asking that the Donatists be punished by depriving them of many of their economic rights—but not of their lives, thus avoiding the production of more martyrs. In response to that petition, but also to other violent acts by the Circumcellions, Emperor Honorius decided that the Donatists were heretics, and that therefore all previous laws against heresy were to be applied to them. The Donatists were to be punished with fines, confiscation of property, imprisonment and even torture—but not death. And no Donatist was allowed to take possession of an inheritance without first becoming a Catholic.

All of this led to a conference convoked by the emperor that gathered in Carthage in 411. Marcellinus, the Roman official presiding over it, was a friend and admirer of Augustine. After long debates about how the assembly was to be conducted, the result was as expected: Marcellinus decided that the laws against Donatists should be applied; he banned Donatist worship and ordered the confiscation of all Donatist properties.

The Later History of Donatism

Apparently Augustine thought that this decision would seal the fate of Donatism, and after that he did not pay much attention to the matter. But the Circumcellions became ever more violent, at a time when the Romans were engaged elsewhere and were less able to make their will obeyed in Africa. A year before the conference in Carthage, in 410, Rome itself had been taken and sacked by the Goths. What was left of the Western empire was now investing all its resources in surviving in Europe. Slowly but inexorably, during the last years of Augustine's life, the Donatists were gaining. By the third decade of the century, it seemed that the Donatists would eventually take the entire Western half of the northern coast of Africa. But then came the invading Vandals, who were at the very gates of Hippo when Augustine died. From that point on, Christianity in North Africa was divided among Catholics, Donatists and Arians—for this was the faith of the invading Vandals. Almost exactly a century after the Vandals, in 533, the Byzantine general Belisarius invaded and conquered the area, and now efforts were made to establish Byzantine Orthodoxy. All of these divisions facilitated the Arab conquests in the seventh century, and there are indications that many of the more extreme Donatists saw the Islamic conquest as a judgment of God against Catholics. But the result of all this was that eventually every form of Christianity—Catholic, Donatist, Arian and Byzantine—disappeared from the area. (Some scholars claim that the deep interest that the Donatists showed in martyrs and their tombs, which was much stronger than in other areas, was a continuation of ancient Berber customs, and that this still continues to this day within the Islamic faith in that area, where rites are practiced in honor of Muslim saints that are very similar to those earlier practiced by the Berbers.)

AUGUSTINE'S VICTORY AND DEFEAT

Augustine's attacks against Donatism, and all his efforts to refute it, did not have the expected success. As soon as imperial authorities, being themselves threatened by the constant menace of the Germanic peoples, withdrew their attention from their North African provinces, Donatism began flourishing anew, and at the end of his days Augustine saw it apparently triumph in most of the region. This was due in great measure to the fact that Donatism was not only a religious or theological movement but also an affirmation of the Libyan identity that the Roman elite tended to ignore or suppress. Augustine does not seem to be aware of this. The clearest indication that he may have understood something about the connection between the cultural and social conflicts of the area and the Donatist schism is his *ABC*, which by its very tone and structure was addressed to less educated readers. But even so, Augustine seems to have been convinced that what was required was a biblical and theological refutation of the opinions of the Donatists, who would then, having been defeated in debate, return to the true church—and even the *ABC* seems to have had the same goal in mind.

The Donatist schism—or, more precisely, schisms, for the Donatists were repeatedly divided among themselves—was not so much a matter of theology as of cultural, social and economic conflicts. As we have seen, in spite of their supposed rigorism the early Donatists were ready to accept into their fellowship some who had clearly been *traditores*. Later, with the Circumcellions, Donatism became a guerilla-warfare movement against everything that was Latin in the interior of the land, and particularly against rich landowners. As to the latter, Augustine does not seem to have understood, as Ambrose had done before him, the pain and injustice inherent in a poor distribution of goods. In a long letter to Hilary, Augustine rejects the Donatist proposition that the rich, by the very fact that they accumulate wealth while others are in need, practice injustice. In this regard, his words remind us of what we often hear when the issue of social justice is raised: "I suspect that some of those who spread about these ideas impudently and imprudently are supported by rich and pious Christians in their needs."[8] While in the preaching of Ambrose there was great stress on the obligation of the rich to share their goods, in Augustine quite often the emphasis seems to be on the obligation of the poor not to lust after the goods of the rich. Thus, while speaking of the attacks of the biblical prophets against excessive riches, he would say, "So now, listen to me, and I will show you that what is condemned in a rich person is not money, but avarice. Look at that well-to-do person standing near you. Perhaps he or she has money, but no avarice, while you have avarice but no money!"[9] This is due in large measure to the emphasis on order that Augustine inherited both from his Latin education and from Neoplatonic philosophy. Thus, commenting on Genesis, he says that

---

[8]*Letter* 157.37. NCP II/3:37.
[9]*Exposition of the Psalms* 51.14. NCP III/17:26.

"there is among humans a natural order in which women are to serve men, sons are to serve parents, and the less intelligent those who are more."[10] He then adds that, although this may not happen in this world, in the end the just who did not follow the perversity of the present will enjoy an eternal and "well ordered" happiness.

It is not only in matters of social injustice that Augustine does not seem to be aware of the depth of feeling among the Berber population, but also in matters having to do with the suppression of their culture. Donatism had become an attempt by the Berber or Libyan population, now subjected to the Romans, to affirm the value of their culture and their traditions. Augustine himself, even though he was a mestizo, had suppressed within himself most of his Libyan roots. In this he was following along the steps of Monica, who, while rejecting Patrick's paganism and seeking his conversion, was making every possible effort to turn his son into a good Roman in everything except his religion.

In short, Augustine's difficulty in seeing the Libyan protest that was involved in the Donatist movement had its roots in his own difficulty in acknowledging the Libyan elements within himself, suppressed by means of a long process of education in which only that which was Greco-Roman was appreciated, and anything that was African in origin was considered barbaric.

On the other hand, while Augustine's work failed in his anti-Donatist efforts, that work did leave a profound imprint on the later course of theology, particularly in matters such as the doctrine of the church and of the sacraments and the use of force in order to suppress or avoid injustice. On this latter point, throughout the Middle Ages the principles that Augustine had proposed for a "just war" were repeatedly used in order to justify the power of the state, and for the use of force and violence—sometimes in forms that Augustine would never have accepted, such as in the Crusades. As to the doctrine of the church, Augustine's teaching regarding the distinction and the unbreakable link between the church invisible and visible became quite common in all later discussions

---

[10] *On the Pentateuch* 1.153.

on ecclesiology. His understanding of the catholicity of the church in terms of its universal presence, in contrast with the regional nature of Donatism, contributed to the confusion between catholicity and uniformity that was prevalent during the Middle Ages. This contributed to the breach between the East and the West. In the times of the Reformation this understanding of catholicity as universality produced an insistence on the use of Latin as a common liturgical language. Even to this day many seem to believe that the catholicity of the church requires that there be uniformity in its practices, customs and rites.

6

The Shepherd and
the Pelagians

None of the many controversies in which Augustine was involved has had a greater impact on later theology than his controversy with the Pelagians. Almost immediately after Augustine's death, the Council of Ephesus condemned Pelagianism. From that point on, very few have accepted the epithet of Pelagian, and most have claimed to be Augustinian. But very few among these supposed Augustinians have really been such, and therefore Pelagius has always had a following, at least on some points of his doctrine.

PELAGIUS

Little or almost nothing is known of the early years in the life of Pelagius. His contemporaries say that he was "British," but it is not clear whether this meant that he came from England, Wales, Scotland or even Ireland. He was born around the year 352, and therefore he may have been just a few years older than Augustine. Nothing is known about his parents, although it would seem that they were relatively learned, or at least that they valued education. The name Pelagius, which means "from the sea," or "marine," is Greek in origin, which seems exceptional for the British Isles, where the overwhelming number of names were of Latin or Celtic origin. Thanks to the support of his parents, Pelagius had a solid education in England. As was usually the case, this education centered on the study of Latin poets and historians—but not of the Greeks, whose writings Pelagius seems to have known only secondhand. When he completed his studies in England, apparently shortly after 380, his parents sent him to study in Rome, where it seems they expected him to make his way in civil service, perhaps as an administrator or as a lawyer. As we shall see, his law studies would later serve him as a model for his theological arguments. Since Augustine went to teach in Rome in 383, while he was still a Manichaean, it would seem that for some time they lived in the same city, although there is no indication that they met. Pelagius remained there until 409, when—apparently fleeing from the Goths, who were approaching the city and would sack it in the following year—he went to Sicily. After remaining on that island for some time he moved to the province of Africa.

All those who knew him say that he was a large man, with wide shoulders and a thick neck, and that his mere presence and his firm and slow gait inspired, if not fear, at least respect. Also, Augustine himself praises his devotion and purity of life—in contrast to Jerome, whose well-known acrimonious language and style reached new heights in his attacks against Pelagius. At the beginning of the controversy, Augustine said that "I read certain writings of Pelagius, a holy man as I hear, and a Christian of considerable religious development."[1] Later, after the controversy had become rather harsh, Augustine summarized his relations with Pelagius as follows:

> Limiting my remarks mostly to my relations with Pelagius, I must say that, when he lived away from Rome as well as when he was in Rome itself, I heard much good about him. Later his own fame made us aware of his debates against the grace of God and even though this notice, which would certainly cause me some grief, was told to me by people I deemed trustworthy, I still wanted to hear it from Pelagius himself or read it in a book of his. I wanted to make sure that if I decided to confront his errors, he would not deny them. When later he came to Africa when I was not here, he came to Hippo. But as my friends tell me he did not proclaim his doctrines and soon left. Then I saw him, I think once or twice, in Carthage, when I was very busy because of a conference we were to hold with the Donatists, but he soon left the African shores.[2]

---

[1] *Punishment and the Forgiveness of Sins* 3.1.1. NCP I/23:121.
[2] *Acts of the Process Against Pelagius* 22.46.

There were few who dared doubt the sincerity or purity of Pelagius; he led the ascetic life of a monastic, although he himself was not a monk in the sense of being a member of a monastic community, but apparently simply led such a life on his own.

It was in 405, when he was in Rome, that Pelagius heard a bishop quoting the words of Augustine in his *Confessions*: "On your exceedingly great mercy rests all my hope. Give what you command, and then command whatever you will [*da quad iubes et iube quod vis*]."[3] These words scandalized Pelagius. "Give what you command and then command whatever you will"? Does this mean that if we do not do something—for instance, if we do not practice continence—th given us the power to do it? Is that not to bla Does it mean that before we practice virtue w us the power to practice it? Is this not to just

Pelagius had a brief altercation with the defended the words of Augustine, and from icizing what Augustine had said about grace and the p of sin—although not referring to Augustine by name, but only to his doctrines and writings. But, as Augustine says in the words quoted above, he did not seek to promote his cause or to convert others to his position, and his criticism of Augustine was moderate. Apparently, Pelagius's main concern was the holiness of an austere life and the theological doctrines that would provide support for such a life. Therefore he did not seek to have others agree with his theological opinions, but did insist that they must lead a holy life.

This was not the attitude of Pelagius's main disciple, Celestius, who also was British, and who was studying law in Rome when he met Pelagius. The latter led him to withdraw from the interests of the world and to devote himself to an austere life in a quest for perfection. Like Pelagius, Celestius never became a monk in the strict sense, but did lead a monastic life in imitation of his teacher. But, differently from Pelagius, Celestius did seek to convince and convert those who did not accept the

---

[3]*Confessions* 10.29.40. NCP I/1:263.

teachings of Pelagius, and he underscored the theological and doctrinal dimensions of those teachings. All of this did not create much reaction or disturbance, even though many found his positions extreme. But when Celestius asked to be ordained as a presbyter it became necessary to examine his theology, and it was then he was accused of being a heretic. Thus it was Celestius's zeal in the diffusion of the teachings of Pelagius, and his desire to be ordained—which would seem to put a stamp of approval on his doctrines—that led a synod gathered in Carthage in 412 to reject his teachings, declaring them to be heresy—which is not surprising, since Augustine was the most respected bishop in the area.

As to Pelagius himself, he traveled to the East and settled in Ephesus. There he was received by Bishop John. But Jerome and others insisted that his teach... A disciple of Augustine, Paulus Orosius, tried to solve the matter, but to no avail. It would seem that the differences were ...tinued until the Council of Ephesus— ...ical Council—condemned Pelagianism ...leath of both Pelagius (who apparently ...3) and then of Augustine (430).

Pelagianism

At the beginning, the debate revolved around the nature of sin as well as its consequences and scope. In the Synod of Carthage in 412, Celestius was accused of teaching that the sin of Adam had consequences for Adam himself but not for his descendants, for all people are born free of sin and remain pure until they sin for themselves. This in turn meant that it was not necessary to baptize infants before they had occasion to commit their own sins. (Note that, while Celestius objected to the baptism of infants, as later the Anabaptists and Baptists would also object, the reason for his objection was different. While today's Baptists oppose the baptism of infants because they are not able to believe and accept the faith on their own, Pelagians opposed that baptism because infants have not yet sinned, and therefore do not need the redemption that baptism offers them.)

As is often the case, what made the debate particularly virulent was not just the conflict regarding the doctrines in themselves, but rather the manner in which each position was manifested in the worship of the church. For a long time it had been customary to baptize the children of believers while they were still in their infancy, and now Celestius refused to do this. On the other hand, there is no doubt it was their interest in the holiness of life that eventually led Pelagius—and then Celestius—to doctrines that are now known as Pelagianism. Thus, among the extant writings of Pelagius there are several that deal almost exclusively with the Christian life and how it ought to be lived. In a letter to a woman by the name of Celesta, Pelagius discusses Christian life in general, and then more specifically the life of a married Christian woman. Its tone is very similar to that of another epistle of Pelagius, *On Virginity*, addressed to a single woman, and his treatise *On the Divine Law*, addressed to an important man of senatorial status who sought to apply the principles of Christianity to his daily life. In this treatise Pelagius focuses on the practical aspects of Christian life, calling his reader to know and obey the law, to remember constantly the reward that has been set aside for him in heaven and therefore to lead a pure and austere life—even though in this treatise there is some reference to baptism and its significance.

In all of this little was said about the grace of God, and what was stressed was the responsibility of the believer. But Pelagius did not seem to stray far away from the teachings of the rest of the church. Proof of this is the fact that his treatises have managed to survive because they were attributed to other respected persons. Ironically, many of them have survived under the name of Jerome, who, while even being a bitter enemy of Pelagius, shared in his ascetic tendencies.

As the debate developed and became ever harsher, the doctrines of Pelagius regarding grace came to be the center of the controversy. The reason why Pelagius reacted so strongly against Augustine's prayer "give what you command, and then command whatever you will" was that this prayer seemed to blame God for human disobedience. Augustine's words would seem to imply that if God does not give us the grace allowing us to do what God wishes, the fault is not ours, but God's. On the other hand, if what we do is to be truly good and virtuous, it must be a product of our own free will, and neither of our nature nor of the grace of God. A stone that falls because that is its nature does not merit condemnation or praise. Nor does a stone that someone throws. In the first case, the stone falls by nature. In the second, by external agency. Likewise, if we sin because of our sinful nature, our actions do not deserve punishment. And if we do good by reason of the grace of God, our actions have no merit.

In all of this argumentation, both Pelagius and Celestius were making use of their background in the study of the Roman legal system. That system stressed the value of law above any other authority. Law was the foundation of all of society, for without it life would be impossible. The task of a jurist was then to apply the law to specific cases, and this was to be done by means of a practical and rigorous logic. In brief, what the jurist was to decide was exactly what the law said, and then how to enforce its obedience. A fundamental part of the process was the principle of possibility—that is, those who cannot obey a law have no obligation to do so, and therefore are not responsible for their lack of compliance. This could be seen specifically in the different ways in which the law was to be applied to free citizens on the one hand and to slaves on the other. Roman laws on slavery were extremely severe, but a slave could not be punished by the civil law for having obeyed what the master commanded. In order to be fully responsible before the law it is necessary not only to have the possibility of obeying but also the freedom to do so or not.

In the writings of Pelagius one immediately notices that he was particularly concerned over the proper administration of law. Pelagius knew well the manner in which the law was abused, frequently in order to subject the less powerful to misery and even death. Given such a situation, the power of the law depended on the justice and equity of the judge, and a capricious judge could not be a proper administrator of justice.

In all of this both Pelagius and Celestius were simply expounding and following the best principles of the Roman legal system, and therefore it is not surprising that Jerome calls Pelagius—perhaps with an ironic tone—"a most Latin man."

When transposed to the field of theology, this meant that in order to be truly just God must judge with equity, and that in order to be a good administrator of law God has to apply it equally to all. Thus, commenting on Romans 2:2, where Paul declares that "the judgment of God rightly falls upon those who do such things," Pelagius says that

> "*the judgment of God against those do such things—rightly falls*" . . . otherwise it would seem that God delights in evil and is displeased by good. But we do know that God shows no favoritism, for God did not even forgive the angels nor God's enemies when they sinned. But human judgment is indeed corrupted in various ways. The integrity of judges frequently bends before love, hatred, fear and greed, and on occasions mercy contends against the rule of justice.[4]

All of this means that merit as well as guilt is to be based on the exercise of the free human will. Those who act according to their own will deserve a reward or a punishment. Those who do so by nature, or moved by God, deserve neither the one nor the other. Indubitably, the grace of God is necessary, because without it we cannot obey the law of God. But since God is a just judge, the gift of grace has to be grounded on a human decision. God gives grace to those who ask for it and deserve it, and not to those who do not ask for it or deserve it. The same is true about the Holy Spirit and the adoption as children of God. Commenting on Romans 8:14, Pelagius refers to "those who are worthy to be ruled by the Holy Spirit." And later, on the basis of Romans 8:17, he declares that "whoever is worthy to be a child is also worthy to be made an heir of the Father and co-heir with the true Son." Just as grace is based on human action and decision, so are the gift of the Spirit and the adoption as a child of God, which are reserved for those deserving such gifts.

All of this was indissolubly joined to the free exercise of the will. If the will is not able by itself to turn toward God and serve God, then there is no merit in such a turning nor in such service. Although exaggerating and in the ironic tone typical of him, Jerome hit the nail on the head in placing on the lips of Pelagius the following words: "I am free of sin. My

---

[4]Pelagius, *Commentary on Romans* 2.2.

clothing is clean. I am ruled by my own will, and therefore I am above
the Apostle. The Apostle did what he did not wish, and wished what he
did not do. But I d⸱   ⸱ lo nothing that my
will does not comm   asm, Jerome places
in the mouth of Pe   ⸱ have said, but that
Jerome claimed w   ⸱mations about the
power of his will a   [he kingdom of God
has been prepare⸱   ⸱tuous life I have prepared it for mysel⸱.

Although the controversy included many other points, this was the
radical difference between Augustine and Pelagius. For the former,
God's law and human corruption are such that a human being is incapable of doing good by their own free will. For the latter, the justice of
God and human integrity are such that a human being is capable of doing
good by their own nature and will. For the former, the grace of God is
not true grace if it is not free—or gratis, *gratia gratis data*. For the latter,
an absolutely free grace would deny the justice of God. These two positions in some ways reflected the experience of each of their two proponents. Pelagius had lived from his very youth a fairly clean and serious
life. From that he had moved on, apparently without great inner
struggles, to an ascetic life, and had devoted himself to follow it and to
call others to the same path. For him, the essence of Christian life was
in an obedience grounded on the free decision of the will. Augustine,
on the other hand, had a turbulent youth, and had shameful memories
of his rebellion against God and of his inability to do as he ought. In
his experience, rebellion against God had roots so deep that they went
into the inner core of the will, so that while Augustine wished to obey
God he found that he could not. Upon looking back on the path that
had taken him to faith, he saw that his corrupt will had not led him to
God until it pleased God to give him the necessary grace for him to
have a new will.

---

[5]Jerome, *Dialogue Against the Pelagians* 2.24.
[6]Jerome, *Dialogue Against the Pelagians* 2.24.

AUGUSTINE ENTERS THE CONTROVERSY

At first Augustine paid scant attention to Pelagius and his doctrines, apparently thinking that here was simply a sincere man with some ideas that were incorrect, but not dangerous. When he had the opportunity to meet Pelagius in Carthage, he had other more pressing concerns, and let that opportunity go by. But the debates that took place in the synod of 412 convinced him that it was necessary to warn his flock on the dangers of Pelagianism, as he did in several sermons. In one of them, dealing with the parable of the pharisee and the publican, he is clearly referring to the Pelagians.

> Let them see now, let them hear all this, those people whoever they are, gabbling away with their impieties, and relying on their own powers; let them listen, those who say, "God made me a human being, I make myself just." Why, you're worse and more detestable than the Pharisee! That Pharisee indeed proudly called himself just, but still he at least gave thanks to God for it. He called himself just; but still he gave thanks to God. . . . What, then must a person be who impiously assails God's grace, if this man is condemned for pride in saying grace?[7]

And since he was aware that the point at which this particular debate most directly touched the lives of his congregation was in worship and in baptismal practices, Augustine immediately moves on to the matter of the baptism of infants, insisting that not even these are completely free of sin.

> And look, immediately after the question at issue has been stated and judgment pronounced, here are the babies coming along, or rather being brought and held up to be touched. Touched by whom, if not the doctor? They're obviously in good health? To whom, then are the infants being held up to be touched? To the savior. If to the savior, then of course to be saved. To whom, if not to the one who came to seek and to save that which was lost? Where had these babies got lost? As far as they are personally concerned, I see them as innocent; I look more deeply for the guilt [that is, to the guilt of Adam].[8]

---

[7]*Sermon* 115.3. NCP III/4:200.
[8]*Sermon* 115.4. NCP III/4:200-201.

Apparently Augustine had no desire to carry the controversy further. For some time he simply continued writing on grace and the need for it without mentioning Pelagius or Celestius. But soon several incidents led him a more belligerent attitude against Pelagius and his followers.

This may be seen, for instance, in the events that took place when a young woman by the name of Demetrias, who had been a disciple of Augustine and of his friend Alypius, decided to devote herself to religious life in perpetual virginity. Her family was so well known in Christian circles that Pelagius as well as Jerome wrote to Demetrias offering advice. Having learned of the letter from Pelagius—and apparently even having it on hand—Augustine and Alypius wrote Juliana, Demetrias's mother, on the dangers of Pelagianism. In that letter to Juliana, Augustine refers to "a book that someone wrote to the holy Demetria," which is certainly Pelagius's letter, and says to her:

> How, then, could we hold back from warning you, to whom we owe so much love, that you should avoid such teachings, since we read the book for the holy Demetrias, and we want rather to learn from your reply who wrote it and whether it reached you. In that book a virgin of Christ might read, if this were not wrong, reasons to believe that she has her virginal holiness and all her spiritual riches from herself alone and in that way, before she has attained perfect happiness, she might learn to be ungrateful to God. God keep her from this![9]

Augustine was being bombarded from several quarters with questions about the teachings of Pelagius and Celestius. Apparently these teachings had gained some following in Sicily, from which a certain Hilary wrote Augustine asking for his advice. Shortly thereafter, also from Sicily, two bishops sent him an anonymous document circulated widely that was evidently written by Celestius. Likewise, he received news from Ephesus about a synod that claimed to have solved the difference, but whose decisions really did not deal with the debated questions, nor did they clarify the meaning of some of the ambiguous phrases of Pelagius.

---

[9]*Letter* 188.2.4. NCP II/3:253.

All of these documents show that, while Augustine believed that the great error of Pelagianism was to regard grace as a gift that was attained through human will and behavior—that is, the error of denying that grace is freely given—for others the questions raising concern were of a more practical nature, and even easier to understand. For instance, Hilary's letter says little about grace. Apparently what concerned him was that Pelagius claimed that the newly born did not already have the stain of sin and therefore did not need to be baptized; that it was possible to live a completely holy life with no taint of sin; that the church could be free of any such taint—in this apparently Hilary is confusing the rigorism of Pelagius with that of the Donatists; that a Christian should never make an oath, even when required by the state; and that the rich who do not give away their wealth are unable to enter the kingdom of God—all of which seems to show that there were several political and social issues involved in the controversy.

The treatise apparently written by Celestius that circulated in Sicily was much more profound, although in it little can be found about grace. The core of the argument of Celestius, which appears repeatedly in the treatise with different nuances, is that for sin to be truly such it must be voluntary, and that therefore it must be possible to avoid it. If it is actually unavoidable, it is not sin. Furthermore, a commandment implies the possibility of obeying it. If it cannot be obeyed, it is not a legitimate commandment. To claim that God gives commandments that we are unable to obey is to say that God is unjust, and therefore is blasphemy. Therefore it is possible to obey the commandments of God through our own will, and thus to live free of all sin.

In all of this one sees once again the foundations of Pelagianism in the Roman legal system. Just as in that system a law in order to be just has to be capable of being obeyed, and in order to be just a judge is not to punish what was unavoidable, God's law is just because it is possible to obey it, and God is just in not punishing anything but that which we say and do out of our own free will and decision.

AUGUSTINE'S RESPONSE

As the controversy grew, Augustine devoted more and more time to it, to the point that a significant portion of his works were now written to refute Pelagianism. His first important writing against Pelagianism was *The Punishment and Forgiveness of Sins and the Baptism of Little Ones*, a work in two books written in 412—precisely when the synod gathered in Carthage was rejecting Pelagianism—in response to a petition of a tribune by name of Marcellinus. According to Augustine, he had already heard rumors about some of these ideas that were being attributed to Pelagius, but had not taken the time to refute them.

> I do not know the source from which this problem has so suddenly come upon us. A short time ago when we were in Carthage, I heard in passing from certain persons, who were casually conversing, that little ones are not baptized in order to receive the forgiveness of sins, but in order to be sanctified in Christ. I was disturbed by this new idea, but since it was not the right moment for me to say something against it and since they were not the kind of persons about whose authority I was concerned, I readily considered the matter over and done with. And now look, it is being defended with burning zeal. See for yourself, it is being preserved in writing: see, the matter has reached a crisis so that we are asked about it by our brethren. See, we are being forced to argue and write against it.[10]

In the first book of this work Augustine deals particularly with original sin and infant baptism. Even though centuries earlier St. Paul had declared that "in Adam all sinned," not all understood this in terms of an inherited sin. In fact, it was in Africa some two hundred years before Augustine that Tertullian proposed and defended that original sin is an inheritance that all receive from Adam. By Augustine's time what Tertullian had said had become part of Christian tradition in practically all the Latin-speaking West—particularly in Africa. Thus, in defending the notion of original sin as an inheritance Augustine was not saying much that was new but simply reaffirming the common faith of the church in his area. It was in large measure thanks to this and several similar writings

---

[10] *The Punishment and Forgiveness of Sins* 3.6.12. NCP I/23:128.

of Augustine that the entire Western church came to think of original sin only in terms of a condition inherited from Adam.

One of the arguments of the Pelagians was that if baptism washes away original sin, the children of believers who have been baptized should not inherit that sin, and therefore they do not need to be baptized. Augustine responds that the inheritance of Adam's sin is such that "the original corruption remains in the offspring in such a way that it makes it guilty, even when in the parents the guilt of that very corruption may have been erased by the remission of sins."[11]

Coming back to the first book of the treatise *The Punishment and Forgiveness of Sins*, Augustine then defends the need to baptize infants in order to free them from the burden of slavery to that original sin. Also in this Augustine was simply repeating and defending what was commonly held by Christians around him.

The second book deals particularly with free will and the possibility of leading a sinless life. In his writings against the Manichaeans, Augustine had underscored the fact that the will is free only in the measure that it is its own cause. Whatever the will decides because of its own nature or as a result of external impulses is not free. Now he finds himself needing to clarify this point, where his teachings could easily be adduced in favor of Pelagianism. For this reason he declares that, although the will is free, there is in every human being a power that opposes good, which Augustine calls "concupiscence"—which is not to be understood always, as it is in common usage, as referring to sexual appetites, but to every earthly appetite that turns the soul away from the love of God. It is because of this concupiscence that human beings are unable by themselves to do any good—or even to wish to do it.

Augustine tries to clarify all of this by means of an example that has become classical in discussions about the relationship between divine grace and human will.

> We are not, of course, helped by God to sin, but we cannot do what is right or carry out the commandment of righteousness in every respect,

---

[11] *On Original Sin* 2.39.44.

unless we are helped by God. The body's eye is not helped by light so that, closed and turned away, it may withdraw from the light; rather, it is helped by it to see, and it cannot do so at all unless the light helps it. In the same way, God, who is the light of the interior human being, helps the sight of our mind, so that we do something good, not according to our own righteousness, but according to his righteousness. But if we turn away from him, that is our fault; then we are wise according to the flesh; then we consent to the concupiscence of the flesh with respect to what is forbidden.[12]

Augustine then turns to the more specific issues raised by Celestius. As to the possibility of not sinning, certainly that possibility does exist, but no one has been able carry it to fruition, for even in the most saintly people concupiscence still has its destructive influence. Later on Augustine would clarify this in more detail.

After sending to Marcellinus this work in two books, Augustine came to know another writing of Pelagius in which the same arguments appeared, although with a different slant. For this reason he added a third book to the two he had sent to Marcellinus.

The treatise *The Spirit the Letter*, written toward the end of 412, was also addressed to Marcellinus, who once again consulted Augustine on some matters that had not been completely clear. This was followed by a long series of works in which Augustine sharpened his doctrine on predestination, and which may be considered as a whole: *On Nature and Grace* (written in 415 in order to refute the book *On Nature* by Pelagius), *On the Grace of Jesus Christ and Original Sin* (418), *On Grace and Free Will* (426), *On Correction and Grace* (427), *On the Predestination of the Saints* (428–429), *On the Gift of Perseverance* (in the same date) and numerous letters and sermons devoted to these various subjects.

Although in the previous sections we have seen some of the matters being debated and how Augustine responded, what made his work particularly important in this regard was the manner in which he progressively systematized grace and its consequences. For this reason he has

---

[12]*The Punishment and Forgiveness of Sins* 2.5.5. NCP I/23:150.

been dubbed "the doctor of grace," and most of the many controversies regarding Augustine's thought and authority have centered on the theme of grace. Therefore it is important to look at Augustine's doctrine of grace as he developed it in response to the Pelagian challenge and as it may be seen in the above-mentioned works.

The first point that must be made clear is that, although there is a difference of emphases between what Augustine said in response to the Manichaeans and the manner in which he answered the Pelagian challenge, he never abandoned or denied what he had said earlier against the Manichaeans regarding free will. The will is free only when it acts out of itself. Whatever one does out of unavoidable necessity is not a free action. Whatever is done as the result of an external force, even though such force may not deny freedom, is still not a free action. In order to be truly free the will has to be able to decide for and by itself.

But the field within which that freedom may work is limited. Thus, for instance, human beings are not able to fly. Their physical freedom is limited to the earth. This does not mean, however, that they are not free, but rather that they are free for certain things and not for others—in this case, they may be free to go wherever they please as long as they do not attempt to fly in the air.

According to Augustine, when Adam and Eve were created they had ample freedom. Since the entire garden was at their disposal, they had freedom not to sin. They could move freely without sinning. But, since in this garden there was also the forbidden tree, they also had the freedom to sin. In short, there was a twofold freedom that included the possibility not to sin (*posse non peccare*) as well as the possibility to sin (*posse peccare*).

All of this changed with Adam's sin. On being expelled from Eden, Adam and Eve were cast out into a world in which they still had ample freedom to determine the course of their lives. But since now humankind was no longer living in the garden in which there was the possibility not to sin, now freedom was limited to the possibility of sinning. In other words, after the fall human beings still have the freedom to sin (*posse peccare*) but no longer have the freedom not to sin. They are now in a state in which they cannot not sin: *non posse non peccare*. This does not mean that there is no longer any freedom, but simply that freedom now has new limits. Just as a human being has full freedom to move over the face of the earth but not to fly away from it, thus a sinner has full freedom to move within the sphere of sin but not to break away from that sphere.

It is important to understand that this does not mean that everything one does is now predetermined, or that one no longer has various alternatives among which to choose. Humans are free, and at every step there are various paths open to them; but all of these paths are sin—just as the many alternatives we have as to where to move along the earth do not include the possibility of simply abandoning the earth and flying away.

It is also important to point out that not all these alternatives are morally equal. Some decisions are better than others. A human being, even after the fall, retains notions of justice, loyalty and so forth. Thus there is still a place for ethics even in the condition of fallen humanity. But even the best ethical decisions are still sinful, for they are actions of a sinful being who does not have the option not to sin. Once again, the only freedom left to the sinner is the freedom to sin (*posse peccare*), but this is a wide freedom, allowing that human being to make decisions, organize life and society, and so on.

Redemption brings about the restoration of the human being, so that now, as in the case of Adam and Eve before the fall, there is both the freedom to sin (*posse peccare*) and the freedom not to sin (*posse non peccare*). This means that believers are now able to make decisions that are not sin, but true virtues. It is within this sphere that Christian life is to be lived. At every step we face a multitude of alternatives. Now some of these are sin, and some are not. Now true holiness is possible. On this point the Pelagians are correct: it is possible to lead a life of perfect holiness. But they are mistaken in believing that such a possibility becomes actual in them or in any other human being besides Jesus. Now it is possible to do good and meritorious works—to which we shall return.

Finally, in the state of glory a human being can no longer sin (*non posse peccare*) but still has the freedom not to sin (*posse non peccare*). Freedom is such an essential element of human life that it remains, even in the kingdom of God, so that even there a redeemed human has alternatives, but none of them is sin—as if in the original garden there had not been a forbidden tree. In his treatise *On Correction and Grace*, Augustine describes the difference between the garden and the final kingdom in terms of the freedom that Adam and Eve enjoyed compared with the freedom of the kingdom.

> It is important carefully and attentively to enquire on the difference between these two things: the possibility not to sin and not having the possibility to sin. . . . The first human being had the possibility of not dying, of not sinning, of not abandoning good. . . . Thus, the original freedom of the will was the possibility not to sin; but the final freedom will far exceed it, for it will be not having the freedom to sin. The original immortality was in being able not to die, the final will be not to be able to die.[13]

But that is not all. If all a fallen human being can do is sin, how can that being move from its present state to that of redemption? The decision to take that step cannot be sin, and therefore is not something the human being can do. Thus, "unless that defect is overcome with the help of grace, no one turns back to righteousness; unless it is healed as an effect of grace, no one enjoys the peace of righteousness."[14]

It is at this point that the grace of God intervenes, giving the human being the possibility of moving from one state to the other and thus restoring the freedom not to sin. Without such grace, human beings in the state of sin cannot pass to the state of redemption, because no matter what they do or what their efforts might be all their decisions are sin. At this point, grace is the power of God acting on human beings in order to allow them to pass from their state of sin to the state of redemption. In refuting Pelagius's treatise *On Nature*, Augustine says it quite clearly.

> But in order to pass to sin, the free choice by which they harmed themselves is sufficient. To return to righteousness, however, they need a physician because they are not well; they need someone to bring them to life, because they are dead. This fellow [Pelagius] says nothing at all about grace, as if they could heal themselves by their own wills alone, because they were able to harm themselves by the will alone.[15]

---

[13]*On Correction and Grace* 12.33.
[14]*The Punishment and Forgiveness of Sins* 2.19.33.
[15]*Nature and Grace* 23.25. NCP I/23:237.

From that point on, grace continues acting in those who are redeemed, now helping them to act in virtue and merit. In other words, grace "begins to operate in us without us so that we may believe, and then co-operates with us."[16]

But there is still another question: How does one explain the fact that some receive this grace and some do not? This is the question that leads Augustine to the doctrines of irresistible grace and predestination. If grace is given to us without any merit on our part, absolutely free (*gratia gratis data*), we cannot say that God gave this grace to some because somehow they merited it and others did not. Granting this grace to some and not to others is an absolutely free action of the sovereign God. It is so free that it is not even grounded on God's foreknowledge about who will believe and who will not. God does have such foreknowledge; but what foreknowledge entails is knowing who will receive saving grace because God has so decided—that is, who are the elect.

Augustine explains this by declaring that, from the point of Adam's sin, all of humanity is a "mass of damnation." God has no need or obligation to forgive anyone. But through the great divine mercy, God decides to choose some and give these that grace that restores to them the freedom not to sin. These elect ones are the totality of those who are to be saved, "those predestined for the kingdom of God whose number is so well fixed that it cannot be added or subtracted."[17] The rest are not condemned because God decides that it will be so but simply because they are part of that sinful mass of damnation which is humanity. Thus those who are not saved are not condemned because God has decided to condemn them, but are simply "abandoned in the mass of perdition by the just judgment of God."[18] God is not being unjust in condemning those who deserve it, nor in granting grace to some among them. "Who but a fool would declare God to be unjust, no matter whether God justly punishes those who deserve or mercifully grants grace to those who do not?"[19]

---

[16] *On Grace and Free Will* 17.33.
[17] *On Correction and Grace* 13.39.
[18] *On the Gift of Perseverance* 14.35.
[19] *Enchiridion* 98.25.

If the number of the elect is fixed, this implies that a person whom God has elected and to whom God has therefore decided to grant grace cannot reject it. On the other hand, this does not mean grace forces the will against itself, but rather that grace transforms it, taking it to the point where it freely decides to receive the grace that is offered to it. Thus in one of his sermons Augustine says:

> Don't regard this violence as harsh and irksome; on the contrary, it is sweet and pleasant. It's the very pleasantness of the thing that drags you to it. Isn't a sheep dragged, or drawn irresistibly, when it's hungry and grass is shown to it? And I presume it is not being moved by bodily force, but pulled by desire.[20]

Thus it is not simply that grace being irresistible forces itself on the will, but rather that grace acts on the will in such a way that it is eventually accepted voluntarily and joyfully. But even so, Augustine's doctrine of irresistible grace and of predestination has been discussed throughout the ages, and has resulted in long and sometimes bitter controversies.

There is, however, another aspect of the manner in which Augustine deals with grace to which theologians have paid less attention, but which has far-reaching consequences. This is Augustine's understanding of grace as a power that God infuses in the human soul so that it may do what God wishes. Before Augustine, when other theologians spoke of the "grace" of God, normally this did not mean a power or an effluvium from God, but rather the goodwill of God, God's forgiving and re-creating love. But following Augustine Western Christianity came to understand grace as a power, and even as a substance that God infuses in the human being—today we would say that it is like fuel that is put into a tank so that an engine may run properly. This is why after Augustine it became customary to speak of various sorts of grace, to classify them and to try to determine the place of each of them in the process of salvation. Thus according to some systems it is necessary to distinguish between "operating" and "cooperating" grace—a distinction that is based on some words of Augustine—or between prevenient grace, regenerating grace,

---

[20]*Sermon* 131.2. NCP III/4:137.

sanctifying grace and so forth. It is also for this reason that after Augustine it became customary to speak of "means of grace," not so much as means that God employs to show grace and mercy but rather as channels through which grace flows. Thus, in baptism, Communion and the other sacraments, a certain measure of grace seems to be injected into the receiver. The believer is to come to these means of grace, not so much seeking the manifestation of the grace of God in forgiveness, but rather to receive a measure of that effluvium of energy, that substance, that is now called grace. For the same reason Latin medieval theologians debated whether grace—this substance that God infuses in believers—is created or uncreated; or, what comes to the same, what difference there is between grace and the Holy Spirit, since both seem to be a power that results in the presence of God within the soul.

BETWEEN TWO CULTURES

It is interesting to note that, while Jerome calls Pelagius a "most Latin man," at least one of the defenders of Pelagianism, Julian of Eclanum, mocked Augustine as "a Punic [that is, an African] exegete," "the Punic Aristotle" and "Sophist of the Punics." Apparently Julian was proud of being a true Italian, from the region of Apulia, in contrast to Augustine, who was an African. Such attacks from Julian would be rather painful for Augustine, who had been a friend of Julian's family for some time and now found himself bitterly attacked by a young man from that very family. This explains Augustine's sharpness when he responds to Julian, who was some thirty years younger than him, as a "brash young man."

The pejorative use of the epithet "Punic"—or "African"—which Julian gives Augustine, which at first would seem to be merely a malicious invective, actually points to an important element in the controversy between Augustine and the Pelagians. As we have seen, both Pelagius and Celestius had been proficient in the study of Roman law, which was the pride of their civilization. Furthermore, one of the claims by which the Romans had sought to justify their colonial enterprises was that through their conquests they were taking to the rest of the world the benefits of their legal and institutional system. Supposedly the colonized people would benefit from the knowledge and application of Roman law, leaving aside their previous barbarism and their capricious governments. Thus, in calling Augustine "the Punic Aristotle" what Julian is suggesting is that the thought of Augustine is not grounded in the order that is characteristic of Greco-Roman thought, but rather in the ancient traditions of the Africans that had been conquered by Rome.

At the very foundation of the Roman legal system stands the supreme authority of law. There are certain principles that exist above every ruler, without which a ruler's government and authority are illegitimate. Certainly emperors and their representatives were not always exponents of this principle; but in that case—in theory at least—their authority would become usurpation. Whoever rules well and properly does not do this according to whim, but according to law, and above all according to the principle of equity that is the foundation of legal order. No ruler, not even the emperor, is above the law.

Pelagius and Celestius—and later their followers and defenders such as Julian of Eclanum—understood God within that frame of reference. God is not above law and equity. Since God is just, the very notion that God condemns all of humankind for the sin of one is inconceivable. This is why Pelagius staunchly opposed the Augustinian doctrine that sin is an inheritance that all humankind has received from Adam, and that makes all of humanity a "mass of damnation." For the same reason, the notion that God chooses some from among that mass of damnation in order to grant them grace and lead them to eternal joy, while abandoning others to suffer the consequences of their sin, is blasphemy, for it implies that God is not just.

This contrasts with the manner in which traditional Punic and Berber cultures understood authority, as we have already seen while dealing with Donatism. For them the chief of the clan or of the tribe did not have authority by reason of the title or function that the law assigned him, but rather in himself. His power and his authority were one, so that he had authority as long as he was able to continue exercising his power, and would lose it if someone else had greater power.

From this perspective, to insist that God must be subject to the manner in which humans understand justice and equity is to deny the power and authority of God. If God is sovereign, it is God who determines what is just. Blasphemy is not, as the Pelagians claimed, in declaring that God is unjust, but rather in attempting to tell God what is just and what is not. And it is precisely this that the Pelagians were doing.

From the perspective of the Pelagians, with their background in Roman law, Augustine's God was unjust and capricious. Augustine the mestizo, while understanding the concern of Pelagians over justice, feels that the Pelagians are trying to limit the power and the authority of God.

Something similar may be said if we look at the controversy from a different perspective. The controversy was not only about the nature of God but also about the nature of humanity. There is no doubt that Augustine, Jerome and all the other main opponents of Pelagianism were so because they feared that Pelagian doctrine would lead believers to be proud of their own salvation, as if it were their work. This may be seen, for instance, in the words of Jerome quoted above in which he says that Pelagius claims to be better than St. Paul. Within the framework of Pelagianism, believers would be able to say that they have believed out of a personal decision, quite apart from the grace of God. Such pride is unacceptable. Believers can never say that they have believed because they were better than those who did not believe, or because they made a better decision, or for any other reason that they can attribute to themselves. A believer's declaration of faith has to be that faith itself has come as a result of the grace of God.

But then there is the concern of the Pelagians. To say that one believes by the grace of God is to say that lack of belief in others is the result of lack of grace, and therefore is also a work of God. This is quite unacceptable. No matter how much Augustine tried to show that he was not blaming God for the unbelief of the reprobate, he was never able to convince the Pelagians that he was not blaming God.

Here again we see the contrast between two cultural backgrounds. From the point of view of Roman law and its vision of an ideal society, the virtue and value of an individual do not depend on their being acknowledged by authority. They are intrinsic to the person, determined by principles that are above the rulers themselves. From the point of view of North African traditions, the virtue and rank of an individual depend on the chief's decision—and when this chief no longer has the strength to make his authority obeyed he is no longer the chief. It is interesting to note that, while in his controversy against Donatism Augustine had recourse to Roman principles of authority, in this other controversy he leans toward North African principles. Both are part of his inheritance. This is precisely the nature of his mestizaje. It is this mestizaje that makes it possible for him to claim resources from one culture or the other, according to various needs and circumstances.

THE CONTROVERSY CONTINUES

While Augustine was still alive there were some who, without being Pelagian, found Augustine's teachings questionable, particularly in what had to do with predestination and the role of the free will in the decision to believe. These people sought an intermediate point that would allow them to balance divine and human action, and grace with free will. For this reason they have been called "semi-Pelagian," although perhaps it would be more accurate to say that they were "semi-Augustinians," for they sought to follow Augustine's doctrine but at the same time to mollify it and make it appear less extreme. We have news of such attitudes first in a monastery in Hadrumetum, fairly close to Hippo. But soon these views became particularly strong in the south of what is today France, particularly in Marseilles, where the very respected monk John Cassian was abbot of the monastery of St. Victor.

The main concern of these "semi-Pelagians" was that Augustine claimed the first step in faith was due only to the grace of God, and not human decision. For the rest, they did agree with Augustine on the centrality of grace for Christian life. They certainly did not wish to take the position of the Pelagians, which had already been rejected by several synods.

The semi-Pelagians also felt that Augustine's doctrine of predestination was shown to be false by the very fact that there are faithful believers who have received grace and yet fall and are lost. If they received grace because they were among the elect, how could they lose it? If the number of the elect is fixed, what can be said about these who fall from grace? Were they not part of that number?

The discussion between Augustine and these semi-Pelagians did not reach the acrimony of his controversies with the Pelagians. In fact, many of these semi-Pelagians addressed Augustine quite respectfully, asking him to clarify his teachings or inviting him to agree with them in their more moderate position.

In any case, these controversies revolved around the matter of the first step in faith (the *initium fidei*). Semi-Pelagians believed this to be the core issue, for it is precisely in affirming that such a first step is to be found only in God that Augustine placed himself in need of affirming a doctrine of absolute predestination on the sole basis of the sovereign decision of God.

This debate was taking place during the latter years of Augustine's life. His two main works on this matter, *On the Predestination of the Saints* and *On the Gift of Perseverance*, were both written in 429, a year before his death—and the second of these is the last of his books.

In both of these works Augustine reaffirms what he has said before regarding predestination, and insists that the *initium fidei* is in the grace of God and not in human will. This must be affirmed, among other reasons, in order to avoid pride among believers.

> Beloved brethren of the Lord, it is necessary to avoid in every way to have humans be proud before God, claiming that they are capable of achieving by themselves what is in fact a promise of God. . . . Do remember that if there is something within us that in some way merits the grace of God that grace would no longer be gratuitous.[21]

As to the case of those who fall after seemingly having received the grace of God, such a thing is impossible, for humans cannot undo the election that God has made. What in truth happens is rather that the person who seemed to have received the grace of God had not actually received it. Perseverance is not a human achievement, but it too is a gift of God, and God grants this gift to those who are counted among God's elect.

---

[21]*On the Predestination of the Saints* 2.6.

We claim first of all that this perseverance which allows one to remain in the love of Christ and of God to the end, that is, until the very end of life—which is the only time in which there is a danger of falling—is a free gift of God. This means that it is impossible to know during this earthly life if one has received this gift or not. If one falls before death, it is said correctly that one did not persevere. How could one claim to have received the gift of perseverance if one did not persevere?[22]

Augustine's death did not put an end to the controversy. In Marseilles, the revered John Cassian declared that "as soon as God sees in us the beginning of a good will, God illumines, stimulates and leads it to salvation. God gives growth to what either God planted or what God has seen sprouting in us as a result of our effort."[23] Thanks to the influence of authors such as Cassian, but particularly to the difficulty in accepting the doctrine of unconditional predestination that Augustine proposed, the controversy raged until the year 529. At that time a synod gathered in Orange declared that the main teachings both of the Pelagians and of the semi-Pelagians were heretical. The first canon of that synod affirms that the sin of Adam affects all humankind, including its freedom; the second, that the sin of Adam affects all his descendants; the third, that God does not confer grace on the basis of human petition. Continuing in the same vein in its twenty-five canons, this council sought to reaffirm Augustinian doctrine. But at the same time the council did not reaffirm Augustine's views on predestination grounded only on the sovereign freedom of God nor his views on irresistible grace. It tacitly seemed to imply that the grace that provides the beginning of faith is the grace of baptism. Within the context of a Christendom in which practically all were baptized, the Augustinian doctrine of a "mass of damnation" lost most of its significance. When, three hundred years later, a monk by the name of Gottschalk tried to revive a radical Augustinianism, he was declared a heretic. This was the beginning of a long series of events through the centuries. In brief, the controversy did not end with the Synod of Orange, but rather continues to this very day.

---

[22]*On the Gift of Perseverance* 1.1.
[23]John Cassian, *Conferences* 13.8.

7

The Shepherd
and the Pagans

While Augustine was seeking to refute movements such as Manichaeism, Donatism and Pelagianism, he was also taking part in the ongoing Christian polemics against paganism.

THE NATURE AND STRENGTH OF PAGANISM

Although today we speak of the traditionally dominant religion in the Mediterranean world as "paganism," the truth is that there was no uniform religion, and that therefore to give a common name to the many existing religions and beliefs is quite artificial. Furthermore, the very word *paganus*, from which we derive the word *pagan*, had little to do with religious matters and was applied to anything that was rustic or uncouth, particularly in rural areas. As one examines it more closely, the religious scene at the time included many forms of religiosity and beliefs that sometimes intermingled and sometimes clashed.

In the first place, one must mention the ancient religions of the Greeks and Romans—the gods of Olympus and the Pantheon of whom the classical poets sang, and which generally were still the core of the official religion of the empire. By Augustine's time, those gods had been generally discredited, not only because of the criticisms of Christians and Jews, but also particularly because of what philosophers and other intellectuals said about them. From long before the time of Christianity, philosophers such as Parmenides, Plato and Aristotle had undermined the ancient traditions about those gods, so it was not only Christians who criticized their anthropomorphism, their whims and their immoralities. If their worship still continued, this was not because they were important in the life of most inhabitants of the empire, but simply because they were said to be the ones who had made Rome great, and therefore it was necessary that they be worshiped so they would continue protecting the empire they had built. Also, those gods were a symbol of the ancient culture, and therefore they had an important place in civil ceremonies, in public buildings, in literature, in the arts and in official festivities.

Both in Rome itself and in the provincial capitals the dominant religion was a vague belief in supernatural powers whose purposes could be discovered by means of divination and astrology, and could also be changed by means of magic and sacrifices. Frequently, before making an important decision officials in the government and generals would consult augers and astrologers who claimed to be able to foretell the future by signs such as the flight of birds, the study of the movements of the heavenly bodies or the analysis of the liver of an animal. Likewise, in order to make certain that these mysterious powers would continue being favorable, they were offered sacrifices, and altars and monuments were built for them.

This may be seen in a letter that Augustine received in the year 390 from the pagan teacher Maximus, in the neighboring city of Madaura—where Augustine had studied.

> Greece tells the story with an uncertain reliability that Mount Olympus is the home of the gods. But we see and approve that the forum of our city is inhabited by a crowd of salutary deities. In fact, who is so demented, so mentally incapacitated as to deny that it is most certain that there is one highest God, without beginning, without natural offspring, the great and magnificent father, as it were? With many names we call upon his powers spread throughout the created world, since we all are ignorant of his proper name. After all, "god" is a name common to all religions. And so it is that, while we as suppliants grasp certain of his members, as it were, piece by piece, in various supplications, we seem to worship him as a whole.[1]

---

[1]*Letter* 16.1. NCP II/1:46.

Among the cultured elite traditional religiosity was often supplanted by what one could call a more enlightened one in which philosophical doctrines took religious overtones and determined the world vision as well as the life of their followers. Such was the case with Stoicism, which had been strongly influential in Rome since the time of Cicero and reached the imperial throne in the second century in the person of Marcus Aurelius. Something similar happened with Neoplatonism, which had been born in Alexandria slightly over a century before Augustine embraced it in the midst of his own intellectual pilgrimage.

There was also a vast variety of religions and beliefs, many of them coming from the eastern zones of the empire and even beyond its borders. One of them was Manichaeism, which has already been discussed because it played an important role in Augustine's religious pilgrimage. Also from Persia came the worship of the god Mithras, which had made particular inroads within the Roman army. From Egypt came Isis and Osiris; from Syria, Attis and Cybele; and from Greece, the Dionysian mysteries.

All these elements intermingled and were confused among themselves, sometimes creating schools, such as the various Gnostic groups, and sometimes simply a diffused and confused religion.

Finally, in the remote agrarian areas there were still many of the ancient beliefs and religious practices that had existed even before the Roman conquests. These varied from place to place, for they frequently included local deities, as well as sacred trees, forests, mountains and other places. It was this type of religion that was first called "paganism" (that is to say, the religion of rustic people); but as time went by and Christianity grew in the cities to the point that the old religions continued existing mostly in the rural zones, the name of paganism was given to the ancient religions in common. By Augustine's time, all that was neither Christian nor Jewish was considered "pagan."

THE DEBATE BEFORE AUGUSTINE'S TIME

This is not the place to review the history of the many conflicts between pagans and Christians that began almost as soon as Christianity entered the scene. These conflicts resulted both in a long series of ever more cruel persecutions, and in apologetic works such as those of Justin, Aristides, Clement and Origen. What was said about Christians, and how they responded, may be read in any history of the church. But among the various criticisms and accusations that were raised against Christianity there was one that came to occupy the center of the debate precisely in Augustine's time. This was the claim that the great disasters of the time, particularly the decadence of Rome, were due to the abandonment of the gods who had made Rome great. This may be seen in the middle of the third century in the persecution under Decius, an emperor who, as part of an entire restoration of Rome and its values, ordered that everyone offer sacrifice before the gods and obtain a document certifying that this had been done. The notion that every disaster was due to the abandonment of the gods, and therefore the Christians were at fault, was common in Africa from a long time before Augustine. In Carthage, toward the end of the second century or early in the third, Tertullian wrote that those who persecuted Christians "justify their ill will by wrongly claiming that Christians are the cause of every calamity or public disaster that appeared."[2] In an attempt to refute such an idea, Tertullian listed a long series of disasters that took place before the advent of Christianity, leading to the conclusion that "if those ancient calamities are taken into account, we see that they are not as many now that God has given the world the presence of Christians, for Christians pray and thus achieve blessings for all, even though the very people who receive the blessings of God attribute them to Jupiter."[3] Likewise, shortly before the time of Augustine, Arnobius, another African, wrote against the notion that after the advent of Christianity the world had become worse, arguing, like Tertullian, that there have always been disasters and calamities.[4] In the third century, a few decades before the time of Arnobius, Cyprian responded to the same accusation by accepting the claim that conditions had worsened, but explaining that what is actually happening is that the world is aging, and that the calamities of the time are nothing but the normal signs of aging:

---

[2]Tertullian, *Apology* 40.
[3]Tertullian, *Apology* 40.
[4]Arnobius of Sicca, *Against the Gentiles* 1.1.

"The world has grown old, and no longer has the energy it used to have. . . . The very decadence of the state is proof of this."[5]

Since these matters had been discussed by many, it is quite likely that Augustine would have said little about them had it not been for the sack of Rome in the year 410.

THE FALL OF ROME

As is usually the case with empires and powerful nations, Rome thought its reign would have no end. How could there be an end to a power that had brought order throughout the Mediterranean basin and boasted that it had brought peace and unity to the entire region? In the middle of the second century, Rome's borders with its traditional enemy, Persia, were well guarded and fortified. The wealth that Roman trade produced had no rival. Under that vast empire everything was well organized and regulated. There were laws for everything, as well as a numerous and well-trained bureaucracy to administer them. This situation was such that some historians have claimed that in the entire previous history of humankind there had been no time as glorious and full of peace as in the Roman Empire at its high point.

But other historians point out that such optimism hid a deep unease. The famous *pax Romana* was not well seen by those who saw themselves as oppressed and exploited. Throughout the imperial period there were constant rebellions in Syria, Egypt, Palestine, Spain and Gaul. There is an echo of this nonconformity with the imperial order in the Revelation of John, which saw the empire as "the beast rising out of the sea" and those who collaborated with it as "another beast that rose out of the earth" (Rev 13:1-8, 11-12). Although these words reflect religious motivations, they also express sentiments widely held in various regions of the empire, and the imperial authorities in turn made every effort to suppress them, for they were a serious threat to the existing order.

There was, however, another threat Romans saw but did not quite understand. Rome had become rich by conquering and pillaging the wealth

---

[5]Cyprian, *To Demetrianus* 3.

of its neighbors. Although Rome claimed and imagined that its wealth was simply the result of its own industrious creativity, the truth is that a goodly part of its wealth came from the lands it had conquered. Roman conquests, first in the rest of Italy, then in Africa, Gaul, Egypt, Spain and even Great Britain, brought to the empire much wealth that the Romans themselves had not produced. If wheat was needed in Italy, it was brought from either Sicily or Egypt. If oil and wine were required, they were brought from Asia Minor or from Spain. If it was tin that was needed, it came from Great Britain. If the population that had been brought into the empire was not satisfied with what it had, it was a matter of conquering new areas and claiming their resources. But by the third century the Roman Empire had reached its greatest extension. It was no longer able to sustain the center by simply extending the borders. To the east, Persia was too powerful to be conquered. The other neighbors were much poorer than the empire itself. Thus military resources that were earlier employed for conquest now had to be devoted to reinforcing and defending the borders of the Rhine and the Danube against the incursions from these other neighbors. This entailed high expenses, but did not bring the wealth that warfare had produced earlier. Thus began a feeling of unease, and this is why in Roman writings of the time one frequently hears the plaint that things were not as they used to be, that the ancient glory was passing.

The difference between one side of the border and the other made the border itself indefensible. On the one side there were peoples—mostly Germanic peoples such as the Goths, Franks and Vandals—who were being hard-pressed by other peoples from the east, and at the same time coveted the wealth of the Romans. On the other side of the border there was a population whose prosperity had accustomed it to a comfortable life and to placing the most onerous tasks on the shoulders of others. With such disparities between the two sides of the border, it was impossible to contain the resulting pressure. Repeatedly the Germanic peoples made military incursions into Roman land, and returned home loaded with booty. Thus the empire that had been built and supported by the booty of war was now threatened by those who were also coming in search of booty. In order to protect its borders, the empire followed the policy of awarding frontier lands to veterans from the army with the hope that, in defending those lands, they would also defend the border. But these veterans were growing older, and their children did not have the same military zeal. Another solution that became quite common but was in itself doomed to failure was to trust the defense of the borders against possible Germanic invaders to the hands of other Germanics who were granted—and sometimes only promised—lands within the borders of the empire on the condition that they were to defend them against possible incursions from their neighbors. Sometimes this worked; but other times—sometimes because the imperial authorities did not fulfill their promises—those who were supposed to be defending the borders turned toward the conquest of Roman territory.

Such conditions had begun to develop during the third century. Early in the fourth, Emperor Diocletian reorganized the defense of the borders, and this led to a period of relative calm and prosperity. This included the reign of powerful emperors such as Constantine and Theodosius. But toward the end of that century the border defenses were increasingly inadequate, with the result that there were constant Germanic incursions into the lands of the empire.

But now conditions had changed. Now those Germanic peoples that earlier had been content with invading the empire, looting its wealth and then returning home with it began to settle within the borders of the empire, sometimes declaring themselves its subjects, but in truth governing themselves, and sometimes in open rebellion.

This process reached its high point in the year 410, when the Visigoths, under the leadership of Alaric, conquered and sacked Rome itself. Such a thing was practically inconceivable to the Romans. Rome, the city that took itself as the capital of the world; Rome, the founder of so many others; Rome, which had called the Mediterranean "our sea," had been conquered and sacked by the supposedly inferior Visigoths.

Soon the word began circulating that it was Christians who were the ultimate cause for this debacle. Rome had been made great by its gods. But now Rome had abandoned them by becoming Christian, and therefore the gods had abandoned it.

AUGUSTINE'S RESPONSE

The alarming news of what had happened in Rome soon reached Hippo, and there too many blamed Christians for it. From the pulpit, Augustine took notice of these opinions by declaring that "it is false what they say about our Christ, that it was he who caused the loss of Rome."[6] And then he turned to an argument based on recent history, reminding his audience that a few years earlier other Goths, servants of the same gods that seemed to have abandoned Rome, tried to conquer it with a much larger army than Alaric's, but failed. And now Rome had fallen to the hands of Alaric, who was an Arian Christian, and therefore did not sacrifice to the ancient gods.

But such a refutation was not enough. It was necessary to offer a wider interpretation of how it was that Rome became great, why it weakened and why the "barbarian" Goths had conquered it. This is the purpose of the great work of Augustine, *City of God.* In essence, the book contrasts two cities, one of God and the other earthly. This was not new, for much of the argument of the book of Revelation in the New Testament is the contrast between the reigning city (Rome, which Revelation also calls Babylon) and the new Jerusalem coming down from heaven. Although it is much more extensive than Revelation, the *City of God* follows essentially a parallel order, for just as Revelation devotes the majority of its earlier chapters to the city of damnation Rome/Babylon and ends with a grand vision of the heavenly city, so does Augustine devote the major part of the early books in this great work to the earthly city and its tragedies, in order to end with the glorious vision of the heavenly city. However, it is not only Revelation that serves as a model and source for Augustine, who had always read and respected Tyconius, one of the most illustrious teachers among the Donatists. From him Augustine took many of the exegetical principles that he expounded in his treatise *On Christian Doctrine.* And Tyconius had written a commentary on Revelation from which Augustine seems to have taken several elements for the composition of the *City of God.* In any case, Augustine did not claim

---

[6]*Sermon* 105.12.

that the theme of the two cities was original. On the contrary, in one of his sermons he says that this is quite commonplace among believers.

> Anyone who is taught Holy Scripture should know where is our citizenship and where we are pilgrims. . . . You have heard and already know that from the beginning of the centuries until their very end there are two cities, now bodily intermingled, but spiritually distinct: one whose goal was eternal life, and is called Jerusalem, and the other whose joy is temporal life, and is called Babylon.[7]

This theme of two cities will be the core of the argument in the *City of God*. But before discussing it one must understand that by a "city" Augustine does not understand exactly what we do today—that is, an urban or metropolitan center. Certainly Rome was a great urban center. But as a "city" it was also an entire social, economic and political order. In other words, what Augustine called a "city" was closer to what we today would call a state or a system of government. (Hence the anomaly that today we do not say someone is a "citizen"—which would normally mean a member of a city—of Paris or New York, which are cities, but of France or the United States, which are not.) Therefore what Augustine will be contrasting are not two metropolitan centers, but two orders, two manners of organizing individual and collective life. This is why Augustine can summarize the entire history of humankind in terms of only two cities, when it is clear that throughout history there have been multitudinous urban centers.

However, Augustine does not limit himself to the narrow subject of the two cities, but proposes to respond to the attacks against Christianity by refuting what pagans say, that evil (particularly the evil that had befallen Rome) was the result of the abandonment of the gods (books 1–5); then arguing that the hope of some pagans to attain an eternal blessedness and joy is false (books 6–10); and finally, relating and discussing some—or rather much—of the course of the history of the two cities (books 11–22).

As this work deals with that entire history it is practically an encyclopedia including much of the history and knowledge of antiquity. Thus already in the second chapter of the first book Augustine begins to write

---

[7]*Sermon* 136.1.

about the Trojan War, then about Roman conquests and then about the fall of Rome, which he reaches in chapter seven. The purpose of all of this is to show that "all that took place in the recent sack of Rome—ruin, blood, rapine, fire, and affliction—is a result of the bellic spirit itself."[8] In other words, Augustine agrees with his Christian African forerunners in declaring that the calamities of his time are no worse than the earlier ones, and that therefore it is not Christians who are to be blamed for them. The true blame resides in the nature itself of nations. From that point he moves on to discuss several of the central themes of theodicy: why there is evil, and particularly why it is that the good suffer jointly with the wicked. But all of this only takes the first fourteen chapters of the first book, and is mentioned here as an indication of the wide scope of the work as a whole. In the next chapter Augustine turns to Roman history in order to deal with Romulus, Lucretia, Cicero, Caesar and a multitude of other figures and events. And at this point we are still in the first of twenty-two books!

Although to the modern reader this enormous work may seem tedious, for the generations that came after Augustine it was a rich mine where they could find the treasures of antiquity. Many of those treasures— historical, literary and even scientific—had been buried with the rubble of the ancient Roman Empire, conquered and destroyed by the Germanic peoples. Yet in the midst of those times of darkness one could always go to the *City of God* as a source not only of information but also of literary inspiration—for many of the early medieval authors sought to emulate it.

It was not until the seventh century, two centuries after Augustine wrote the *City of God*, that the *Etymologies* of Isidore of Seville became another source for similar knowledge of antiquity. The *Etymologies* had the advantage that in them everything was discussed in an orderly fashion, within a clear outline, while in the *City of God* it was difficult to see the logical order of the hundreds of arguments, examples and topics that Augustine offers. But even so, much of the information found in Isidore was taken from the *City of God*, and—thanks in part to the

---

[8]*City of God* 1.7.

prestige of its author—the *City of God* always had wider circulation than the *Etymologies*. Toward the end of the eighth and early in the ninth centuries, Charlemagne frequently requested that the *City of God* be read to him—apparently because he had the dream of turning his empire into an incarnation or at least a reflection of the heavenly city.

But the *City of God* was much more than an encyclopedia. It was also an entire philosophy of history. How was one to explain the rise and fall of nations and empires? Should it be seen as a result of the conflict among gods, as seemed to be the case in the *Iliad* and in other Greco-Roman literature? Could it be that when a people abandons the gods that made it great these gods in turn abandon it, as many pagans were saying after the sack of Rome? Could it be that the easy life of the powerful leads to their own destruction? Could it be that in fact there is no order in history or in life, but only chaos and whim? Is there something intrinsic to power itself that leads to its own dissolution?

Augustine's response is that all the great civilizations are simply expressions of a single city, of a single way of ordering life and social relations. The inevitable failure of every empire is due precisely to that fact: that it is simply a manifestation of the "earthly city."

The gist of Augustine's argument is to be found at the end of book fourteen in this work of twenty-two books—that is, very near the center of the work, so that from this point on the preceding fourteen books seem to be a mere prologue or announcement of the main theme. Augustine expresses it as follows:

> Two loves founded two cities. The love of self to the point of neglecting God founded the earthly city. And the love of God to the point of neglecting self founded the heavenly one. The first glories in itself, and the second glorifies God above everything else. The first boasts of its own glory, and the second says to God: "You are my glory and it is you who allow me to hold my head high." The first rules over the princes and the nations that it has subjected under the impulse of the concupiscence for power. In the second, all serve one another in mutual love, the rulers advising and the subjects obeying.[9]

---

[9] *City of God* 14.28.

It is on the basis of this main thesis that Augustine builds his entire narrative and review of human history. In that history the two cities are intertwined: the earthly and the heavenly, the one built on love of self and the other built on love of God. These two cities have existed in parallel and have been intermingled throughout history, and that condition of intermingling and of conflict will continue until the final consummation, when the earthly city will disappear and the heavenly will prevail.

However, this must not be stated in terms of an absolute contrast, as if there were only evil in the earthly city and only good in the heavenly. Such an interpretation would be close to the Manichaean dualism against which Augustine struggled throughout his life. As Augustine reaffirms in the *City of God*, "There is a nature in which there is no evil, in which there can be no evil; but there can never be a nature in which there is no good."[10] For this reason there are at least two things that the two cities have in common. The first is that both are based on love. They are two different loves, the one directed toward self and the other toward God. Even though its object may not be the proper one, love is the foundation of all human life. This is the great truth to which Augustine referred at the beginning of his *Confessions* when addressing to God his famous words: "You have made us for You, and our heart will be restless until it rests in You."[11] This means that the error in the earthly city does not consist in loving, but rather in loving the creature above the Creator. Even in the midst of the earthy city, human beings seek a good, even though what they seek is not the absolutely good, and in any case it is not where they seek it. This is true, for instance, of peace, which all seek, for even war—at least supposedly—is waged so that there may be peace. But "the peace of sinners, when compared with the peace of the just, does not even deserve to be called peace."[12]

Second, the two cities have in common the very fact that they are "cities"—that is to say, social orders. Augustine does not understand Christian life, either in this world or in the next, as a solitary life in the

---

[10]*City of God* 19.2.
[11]*Confessions* 1.1.
[12]*City of God* 19.12.3.

sole presence of God, but rather as community life, as part of a society. Augustine agreed with Aristotle's much earlier definition of a human being as a "political animal"—or perhaps more literally, as an "animal of the city"—and truly wise life he saw as life in community. This is true not only of the earthly city but also of the heavenly. "If the life of the saints were not social, where would the heavenly city begin? How would it develop and how would it reach its end?"[13] Therefore, although the visible church is not the same as the heavenly city, it is not possible to be a citizen of the eternal city without participating in its manifestation here in the present life, even in the midst of the earthly city.

This in turn means that Christians cannot abandon or lose interest in the earthly city in which they are presently living. Although their citizenship is in heaven, Christians must certainly grieve over all the sufferings and tragedies that have resulted from the sack of Rome. As we have seen, Augustine himself intervened repeatedly in the surrounding society, seeking justice and peace, and even appealed to the temporal power to suppress the activities of the Circumcellions.

In a way, what Augustine does in this passage, as in most of this great work, is to interpret the history of humanity in the light of his own history. In his *Confessions*, Augustine speaks about the agony of that "struggle within my soul, of me against myself."[14] Now that struggle is translated to the cosmic level, as a great conflict between two wills, between two loves that vie for the love and the life of humankind: the love of God and the love of self. And these cosmic dimensions of the two cities born out of these two loves go back even to the time before the creation of the world, for they may be seen in the conflicts between the good angels and those that fell.

However, as we have repeatedly seen, Augustine's internal conflict was not only a conflict between willing and not willing, or between willing the good and willing the evil, but also between the Roman and the African in him, between Monica's faith, which he learned in the cradle, and Patrick's culture, which he learned in the schools. His conversion was

---

[13]*City of God* 19.5.
[14]*Confessions* 8.12.27.

based on the possibility of living Monica's faith within Patrick's culture. When confronted with the Donatists, he opted for Roman traditions in which authority was grounded on the office more than on the behavior of a person. He preferred this over the African traditional view, in which authority was derived from one's behavior—and, in the case of church leaders, from holiness. Later, when facing the Pelagians—who quite correctly pointed to his "Africanness"—he took the opposite option, arguing that the authority of the sovereign God does not depend on God following human notions of justice. Now, before the Roman debacle, while he grieves over it, he blames not only the Gothic invaders but also the Romans themselves. In reality, believers in Christ are not citizens of Rome or of the Visigothic nation—both of which are expressions of the earthly city—but rather have a different and higher citizenship.

On this point, Augustine joined a long tradition going back at least to the time of Paul, who even though he was a citizen of both Rome and Tarsus had declared that "our citizenship is in heaven" (Phil 3:20). Among the apologists, Aristides had affirmed that believers in Christ are a different race than the rest of humankind, for they are neither Jews nor Gentiles. Tatian had rejoiced, trying to show the superiority of the religion and wisdom of the "barbarians" above those of the Greeks. Now Augustine combined all of this with his own mestizaje—he, who was both African and Roman, and therefore both and neither one nor the other—in order to develop a philosophy of history, a vision of God's action, that did not depend on Roman civilization, and in which even the Visigoths had a place.

That mestizo vision was one of the factors that allowed Augustine to serve as a bridge between the Greco-Roman past that was waning and the new regime that was dawning—a regime of disorder, obscurantism and violence, from which eventually, as a new incarnation of the earthly city, Western civilization would develop.

8

Augustine as a Lens for Western Christianity

It has repeatedly been said that Augustine is the bridge connecting the medieval church with the ancient, and that therefore he is also a bridge connecting us with that church of the early centuries. Without him, much of the intellectual inheritance of antiquity would have been lost, or in any case would have remained forgotten in obscure libraries, awaiting its discovery. It was he who gave the pastors and other church leaders of the Middle Ages the intellectual tools that they employed in the difficult task of leading the life of the church in those insecure and obscure times.

In more specific terms, Augustine's insistence on the power and initiative of grace was a corrective in the midst of a church that was turning increasingly legalistic, as if God were no more than the inexorable judge meting out rewards for the good and punishment for the wicked. It was with just cause that Augustine came to be known as "the doctor of grace." In this, he helped preserve the message of love and grace that is at the very heart of the gospel, and he served as a guide for the interpretation of the sacred text—particularly the epistles of Paul.

Also, in the years that immediately followed his death, Augustine was a reminder to the entire church that, even in the midst of the reigning obscurantism, the greatest commandment includes loving God with all the mind. His entire work could be seen as a great bridge not only between the ancient and the newer times but also between what is known by means of the gospel and Scripture and what is known because God illumines the mind of every human being. It was Augustine who brought to Latin-speaking theology what had been said by earlier Greek writers such as Justin: that there can be no contradiction between what God teaches us through reason and what God teaches us through revelation. Thus thanks to Augustine the ideas and some of the writings of Plato and his disciples continued being used by theologians.

But in serving as a bridge Augustine also left his imprint on the traditions and ideas that he transmitted, and therefore in some ways he also became a lens or filter that made it very difficult to approach Christian antiquity in any other way than through him. In consequence, while Augustine transmitted antiquity to the Latin-speaking medieval church, he also transmitted an antiquity interpreted and selected by him.

The clearest example of this is the lack of knowledge of the ancient Greek writers in the medieval Latin West. Augustine himself says that, although in his youth he did study some Greek, he was never attracted by that language. Therefore his theological readings consisted mostly of Latin authors, and of a few Greek writings that had been translated into Latin—for instance, the treatise *On the Holy Spirit* by Basil the Great, which Ambrose had translated and adapted for the Latin-speaking church. The resultant loss was significant. Important and enlightened ancient authorities such as Irenaeus, Clement of Alexandria, Origen, Athanasius, Gregory of Nyssa, Gregory of Nazianzus and many others were practically forgotten in a Western Christianity that learned Christian antiquity through the lens of Augustine.

This had significant consequences. As I have tried to show in another essay, in the Eastern and Greek-speaking areas of Christianity there was a type of theology that differed from the vision of North African theologians such as Tertullian, Cyprian, Arnobius and others.[1] Thanks to Augustine, the type of theology that prevailed in North Africa also became dominant throughout the Latin-speaking West. This was one of the reasons why Western Christianity had a marked tendency to see God primarily as a legislator and a judge, and to see Christian life as a constant

---

[1] See Justo L. González, *Christian Thought Revisited: Three Types of Theology* (Maryknoll, NY: Orbis, 1999).

struggle to merit eternal life. Within that tendency, Christian life was paying for the debt contracted by sin. If baptism erases that debt, what is one to do with sins that are committed after baptism? In response to that question the entire penitential system developed that eventually would lead to the sale of indulgences and to the Protestant Reformation.

This leads us to the much-debated question of whether Augustine was a forerunner of the Reformation. Roman Catholicism has always insisted that its teachings regarding salvation are the same as those of St. Augustine. But at the same time, both Luther and Calvin repeatedly affirmed that their claims were supported by Augustine. In fact, Augustine is the theologian most frequently quoted by both Reformers.

Protestants have had good cause to appeal to Augustine, the "doctor of grace," in quest of support for their insistence on justification as a work of God, and not as a human work. As Augustine had said, in order really to deserve the name of grace, grace must be absolutely freely given— *gratia gratis data*. There can be no previous conditions or requirements. There is no way of gaining or meriting grace. On that basis Augustine developed his doctrines of predestination, of the fixed number of the elect and of the impossibility of falling from grace that later found echo in the Calvinist Synod of Dort and in the Westminster Confession.

But there is another element in the manner in which Augustine deals with salvation that is diametrically opposed to Protestantism. Although it is true that the beginning of faith is in the grace of God, and that this is totally unmerited, salvation is still attained by the merit of good works. As Augustine understood matters, the grace of God operates in the elect before they are able to have the freedom not to sin; but thereafter that grace cooperates with them so that, by means of the new freedom that they now have not to sin, they may acquire the merits that will lead them to eternal life. Thus, in the famous debate as to whether salvation is through the unmerited grace of God or through the merit of works, Augustine would say that it is the unmerited grace of God that makes us capable of acting in such a way as to merit salvation. (Which is the reason why it was later necessary to create doctrines such as the existence of purgatory, which is the place where those who are to be saved go when

they die if they do not have sufficient merit, as well as limbo, the desti-
nation of the innocents who die before being baptized, and the treasury
of merit, which serves to supply the lack of merit of those who seek
shelter under the penitential system of the church.)

In large measure, the entire debate is a result of the lens through which
Augustine taught us to read the gospel. If, as Augustine and his type of
theology lead us to believe, sin is a debt that must be paid, then the
debate has to do with how that debt is to be paid—whether by the work
of Christ alone or by that work joined with human merit. In looking at
the gospel as merely the good news that the debt has been paid or can be
paid, both Tridentine Catholicism and orthodox Protestantism have
limited their vision to what may be seen through the lens of Augustine.

Finally, it is also to Augustine that we owe the great impact of Platonism on Christianity, particularly until the thirteenth century. In
making use of Platonic philosophy, Augustine was able to show to the
entire Western church that reason does not contradict faith. This was and
still is a valuable point to remember. But by understanding reason and
its processes in Platonic terms, Augustine discounted the importance of
what is learned through the senses, which can only lead to the knowledge
of passing things. This in turn led Western Christianity to undervalue
observation as a means to know truth—at least until the thirteenth
century, when the rediscovery of Aristotle in the work of Albert the
Great and Thomas Aquinas opened the way to observation, and eventually to experimentation.

Augustine's Platonism may also be seen in the *City of God*. There he
finds a place for the secular history of the earthly city, which is manifested in states, kingdoms and empires. But when the end comes all that
will be important will be the city of God and its history. The other, secular
history, will simply be erased—which is confirmed by Augustine's strange
notion that in eternal life we shall have no memory of anything in this
life that was marked by sin. In the end, the history of the world, the
history of the earthly city, has no significance.

Today many theologians rightly doubt that division of history in two—
the history of the world and the history of salvation—and insist that

God's work of salvation takes place through the entirety of human history, and that therefore that history is the proper field of action for Christians.

In all of this we may see how Augustine, while being a bridge, is also a lens. As a bridge, he puts us in contact with Christian antiquity. As a lens, he leads us to understand that antiquity in a certain way. Without the lens, we would not be able to see. But if we use only that lens, there will also be much that we will not see or will not understand.

Finally, if it is true that his own mestizo background helped Augustine in his spiritual and intellectual pilgrimage and left an imprint on his entire theology, one may ask if that very mestizaje was not part of what allowed Augustine's theology to make headway as the new mestizaje was developing precisely at the time of Augustine's death: the mestizaje between the Greco-Roman and the Germanic, which eventually gave birth to Western civilization and to theology within that civilization. Such a thing should not surprise us, for throughout history great theological movements have taken place in what we might well call spheres of mestizaje—including the Hebrew-Gentile mestizaje that gave birth to the New Testament, and the Greco-Roman mestizaje that was the cradle of early Christian theology.

If that is the case, the theology and experience of Augustine may well help us attain a deeper understanding of the gospel precisely by reason of the mestizaje in which we live and which has formed us. Whether we realize it or not, all cultures and civilizations have arisen out of various forms of mestizaje—the Greco-Roman mestizaje, the Latin-Germanic mestizaje, the Saxon-Norman mestizaje, the Iberian-Amerindian mestizaje. Throughout history there have always been many who seemed to believe that mestizaje is an obstacle to progress, and that a civilization's task is to preserve its purity. Obviously, such people forget the various mestizajes that have led to their present culture. And most importantly, they also forget that what was true of individuals such as Augustine, and has been true of every culture and civilization, is still true today: that very mestizaje some see as a sign of shame, and some would try to forestall or to deny, may well be a sign of the future from which God is calling us.

Index

Finding the Textbook You Need

The IVP Academic Textbook Selector
is an online tool for instantly finding the IVP books
suitable for over 250 courses across 24 disciplines.

www.ivpress.com/academic/